BRAHMO SAMAJ AND NORTH-EAST INDIA

BRAHMO SAMAJ AND NORTH-EAST INDIA

DIPANKAR BANERJEE

ANAMIKA PUBLISHERS & DISTRIBUTORS (P) LTD.
4697/3, 21A, Ansari Road, Daryaganj
New Delhi 110002
Phone: 2328 1655

First Published 2006

ISBN 81-7975-176-7

PRINTED IN INDIA

Published by Anamika Publishers & Distributors (P) Ltd., 4697/3, 21A, Ansari Road, Daryaganj, New Delhi 110002. Typeset by VGA, VP-216A, Pitampura, Delhi 110088 and Printed at Nagri Printers, Delhi.

To

my inspiration

Professor Sabyasachi Bhattacharya

for always being there

and believing in me

CONTENTS

FOREWORD

It is quite well-known that the Brahmo Samaj had played an important part in the regeneration of modern India from its inception in 1828 to its development into an all India movement in 1866. The ideals of the Samaj carried to North-East India by a group of Assamese elites, who studied in Calcutta, created ripples in the socio-cultural life of this region. Many branches of the Samaj were set up in different parts of the Brahmaputra valley by the end of 1883. This movement also entered the Khasi Hills. The Brahmo emissaries of Bengal had an important role in the socio-cultural regeneration of Assam. Depending on the unexplored primary and secondary sources the author of this work has developed the narrative thematically in three chapters and has thrown interesting light on 'this lesser explored field of research' with the idea of giving 'a more comprehensive picture of the Brahmo Samaj activities and its impact in North-East India'. There is no doubt that in this work Dr. Dipankar Banerjee has made a very valuable contribution to our knowledge of the Brahmo movement in this part of our country.

Rammohun Roy, founder of the Brahmo Samaj, initiated the simple message of Divine Unity. Devendra Nath Tagore gave to the Samaj the 'Covenant for the future Communion'. Under Keshub Chunder Sen the Brahmo Samaj became 'an all India movement and a power in the land'. But "with the gradual progress of the Samaj, differences in views and opinions have made their appearance". However, the Samaj could initiate a movement to fight the battle for freedom on all fronts—social, moral, economic, educational, political and religious. The path for the founder-father of the Samaj was not at all a rosy one. In an address delivered at the 'Brahmobandhu Sabha' on 26 Baishakh 1271 B.S. Devendra Nath Tagore said that Rammohun Roy was vehemently opposed by the orthodox Hindus, Christians and Muslims when he tried to introduce a new meditation prescription for one God with the help of religious book of each community.

With the *bhakti* upheaval in the Brahmo Samaj at Monghyr from 1867 by Keshub Chunder Sen two distinct trends of thought engulfed it. On the one hand there was "a great spirit of discontent with the old theology and an earnest struggle to realize a better order of things". On the other hand, "there was a distrust of things that favoured of the higher realms of the spirit,—a relentless rationalism which placed the worship of the intellect above everything else". It is to be noted that during this time great changes took place in the world. Religion and spirituality 'seemed to have fallen into disrepute'. The human mind was then 'plunged into the vortex of materialism'. The writings of Darwin, Spencer, Mill, Huxley and the like agitated very much the public mind. The atmosphere outside the Brahmo Samaj in those days was 'surcharged with rationalism'. It also influenced the Brahmo Samaj. Thus "side by side with the *Bhakti* movement there was a counter-movement of Rationalism which threatened to impede and dislocate the natural upholding of spirituality in the new community" of Keshub Chunder Sen.

Founding the Bharat Varshiya Brahma Mandir at Calcutta on 22 August 1869, for regular public worship harmoniously blending 'the Hindu, the Gothic, the Buddhist and Saracenic styles of architecture', which was 'a symbol of reverence of all faiths', Keshub Chunder Sen proclaimed: "All mankind will unite in a Universal Church; at the same time, it will be adapted to the peculiar circumstances of each nation and assume a national character". But his efforts to build up a new human society bringing closer of different religious groups were not successful. Referring to Keshub Chunder Sen's 'doctrine of one

Church for all mankind', Sarvapalli Radhakrishnan in a 'Foreword' to *Biography of a New Faith*, Volume Two by Prosanto Kumar Sen observed on 22 February 1954: "Today when humanity is broken up into different compartments each professing a different religious tradition, we cannot hope to develop psychological unity and spiritual coherence essential for a world community". Radhakrishnan also commented: "It is said that to be born in a church is good but one should not die in it. The dogmas and rites, the forms and prayers which are prescribed by a religious organisation are a means to an end but not the end it all. Life becomes easy if we follow established usage and conform to general practices but this ease is acquired at the expense of personal integrity and authenticity". Again, Radhakrishnan said: "If the Brahmo movement today does not seem to be flourishing, it is because its fundamental motives have been accepted by Hindu society".

Dr. Dipankar Banerjee rightly pointed out that the "Brahmo Samaj activists in their own way were able to create a positive socio-cultural impact" in North-East India. Without controverting it, one may ask, then, why the Brahmos in Assam were 'microscopic in terms of number' and remained confined to an upper stratum elite? Perhaps we would find the answer in the deep-rooted socio-cultural movement initiated by Sankaradeva and his disciples. In this situation it became difficult for the Brahmo Samaj to make an inroad into Assam. Sivanath Sastri in his addresses delivered by him as the President of Theistic Conferences at Calcutta in 1906, at Coconada in 1907 and at Allahabad in 1910 (published in the form of a monograph under the title *Theistic Church in India* in 1966 from the Sadharan Brahmo Samaj) admitted: "The last but the most important part of our work, as preachers of a new faith is to device means for effective propagation. The efforts we have made in that direction up to this time are but few and feeble. The field lying before us is extensive. Not to speak of other lands, where the light of the new faith should be taken, for it is certainly a world-religion, vast masses in the country are lying near at hand who have not yet heard of the new message. Our efforts have been up to this time, chiefly confined to a limited number of educated people in whom the faculty of reverence has been partly destroyed by a system of foreign education. We are crying at their door, but even they have not listened to us". In this circumstance the cry for 'one God, one Church, one Law and one Humanity' could not draw the attention of a large number of people.

There was no doubt that the Brahmo Samaj movement was 'pre-eminently a movement of social and religious reform'. But "it has nonetheless been really the first and the most powerful political force in modern India also". It was Rammohun Roy who "persuaded Lord William Bentinck to decide in favour of Western learning even against the recommendations of the Court of Directors". Indians trained 'in modern learning and criticism' played notable part in the struggle for freedom. Bipin Chandra Pal in his monograph entitled *The Brahmo Samaj and the Battle for Swaraj* (new edition, Calcutta, May 1945) wrote that the Brahmo Samaj "had stood up from the days of Raja Ram Mohun Roy for complete personal freedom". Bipin Chandra Pal also said that "What Martin Luther did in Christiandom, the Raja tried to do in modern India, or even more correctly speaking, in the modern world". He wrote that Sivanath Sastri as minister of the Sadharan Brahmo Samaj introduced a special prayer during the congregational worship of the Samaj 'for the special uplift and emancipation of his own country and people'. Bipin Chandra Pal stated that "the Brahmo Samaj was among the very first to contribute to this inspiring hymnology of the present nationalism and freedom movement in India". Earlier patriotic hymns or national songs were composed by members of the Brahmo Samaj. Satyendra Nath Tagore, Jyotindra Nath Tagore and Govinda Chandra Roy 'were the authors of the most favourite of the first batch of these national songs'. Bipin Chandra Pal said that "Sivanath Sastri was the first to introduce patriotic songs into general hymn-book of the Samaj". Surendranath Banerjea preached 'a new gospel of political freedom' and formed 'political societies among the youthful intellectuals of Calcutta'.

Sivanath Sastri dreamt of "a commune of religio-political workers who would devote themselves absolutely to the service of their country aiming at the complete emancipation of the people from all forms of bondage, theological and sacredotal, social and economic as well as political". In this monograph Bipin Chandra Pal highlighted the direct and indirect contributions of the Samaj 'to the political freedom or the Swaraj movement in India'.

Dr. Dipankar Banerjee has drawn our attention to the fact that the forward looking Assamese elite were influenced in various ways by the Brahmo Samaj movement. The scholars engaged in studying the socio-cultural history of North-East India would certainly welcome this work as an important addition to the history of this movement in this region.

18 April, 2006

AMALENDU DE
Former President
The Asiatic Society, Kolkata

PREFACE

In August 2001 I was approached by Dr. Basana Ranjan Halder, President of the Board of Trustees of Gauhati Brahmo Samaj, to deliver the keynote address at the inaugural session of the 111th Session of the All India Brahmo Conference. As the Conference was to be held at Guwahati for the first time, the organizers expected me to speak on the subject: Brahmo Samaj and North-East India.

I honestly told Dr. Halder that I did not have any access to the subject. There were many learned scholars of the region who might have done better justice to the same. But Dr. Halder insisted that as there was practically no record available on the early Brahmo Movement in the North-Eastern region, pettiest of the effort in this regard would be a welcome contribution. That is how this study was initiated.

As I was preparing for my address, I understood that not only the records related to the subject were difficult to trace in Assam, but many of the Brahmo Samaj properties including old Brahmo prayer halls in North-East India had also been lost to the posterity. I gradually realised that though the total number of people who followed the Brahmo faith was microscopic, the Samaj played quite an important role at a certain period of history of the region. However, its historic role has not as yet been properly assessed. After I delivered my address (it contained only nine pages) at the Conference, I was overwhelmed and touched when Lt. Gen. S.K. Sinha, PVSM, Hon'ble Governor of Assam (who is also a historian by his own right) referred to my address several times in his inaugural address of the Conference. He suggested that the records related to the Brahmo Samaj in the North-East ought to be documented. Many delegates from Calcutta and South India, including the representatives of the Unitarian church asked me to undertake further study on the Brahmo Samaj in North-East India. That was a great inspiration for me.

Since then the officials of Gauhati Brahmo Samaj kept reminding me that I should take up a more detailed study on the subject. Unfortunately, I could not honour their request immediately and I took a long time to start the study as I had some other pressing assignments including two visits abroad in between. I wish I would have got some more time for a more elaborate study—particularly on the role of Brahmo Samaj in respect of labour problem of Assam. This, however, is not an excuse for my lapses and transgressions.

Various reform movements of the nineteenth century were the principal forces for social awakening in India. It is an accepted fact that the Brahmo Samaj was to a great extent responsible for bringing that awakening and social change in the country. Though it started in Bengal, it gradually spread over to other parts of India. But how this Brahmo Samaj movement spread to the remote corners of the country as well as the neighbouring provinces has remained relatively a barren field of research. This study attempts to throw some light on this important but unexplored field of research.

The Brahmo Samaj movement in the North-East was basically confined to the Barak valley, the Brahmaputra valley and the Khasi Hills. Khasi Hills was a part of Assam till 1970 and in the fitness of things, an appropriate title of this book should have been Brahmo Samaj and Assam. However, keeping in mind the consequent formation of the state of Meghalaya and in tune with the original subject of the key note address, the book has been titled *Brahmo Samaj and the North-East India*. Data and materials for this work have been collected from different sources. Newspapers like *Brahmo Public Opinion, Sanjivani* and *The Indian Messenger,* which I have consulted at Brahmo Samaj Library, Kolkata and in the newspaper section of the National Library Kolkata need immediate preservation, and more importantly, should be immediately microfilmed. Though some old libraries at Shillong had lots of rare books on the subject, almost everything had been destroyed or lost permanently during the last few decades. However, I have tried to consult as much as possible, though I sincerely believe that there is scope for more serious research on the subject.

Dept. of History
Gauhati University
Guwahati 781014
Assam, India

DIPANKAR BANERJEE

ACKNOWLEDGEMENTS

I am grateful to Dr. B.R. Halder, President, Board of Trustees, Brahmo Samaj, Guwahati who stimulated my interest in Brahmo Samaj movement in North-East India. He constantly encouraged me to undertake this study which remained a barren field of research.

I must sincerely acknowledge with thanks the minor research project grant that has been provided to me by the Indian Council of Historical Research, New Delhi to undertake a part of this study.

I owe my deep gratitude to Prof. Amalendu De, former President of the Asiatic Society, Kolkata and a historian of repute for writing the foreword of the book which has immensely enhanced its value.

The management of Anamika Publishers and Distributors (P) Ltd. also need to be thanked immensely for the interest they have shown in the publication of this book.

In fact, for this study, my debts are many: to Prof. Amalendu Guha and Prof. J. B. Bhattacharjee who have been kind enough to go through the manuscript and provided valuable inputs; to Krishnanjan Chanda of the South Point School, Guwahati, for his support; to Monideepa Chowdhury, and Devasree Datta of Silchar Women's College for sharing my load; to Anjali Lahiri for making available to me some rare books; to late Santi Ranjan Dasgupta of Dhubri, Indira Khuslani of Kolkata and Susama Roy of Shillong for their valuable interviews; to Nirupama Bargohain and Anima Guha for their suggestions; to the officials and staff of Brahmo Samaj libraries of Kolkata, National Library Kolkata, Dept. of Historical and Antiquarian Studies, Guwahati and ICHR NE Regional Centre, Guwahati; Ramesh Prasad Agarwalla and Sankar Lall Agarwalla for their encouragement; to my wife Purabi and daughter Emon for arranging the materials; to Gautam Chowdhury for handling the computer work; to my son Tirthankar Banerjee for designing the cover. I take this opportunity to thank them all.

Dept. of History
Gauhati University
Guwahati 781 014
Assam, India

DIPANKAR BANERJEE

INTRODUCTION

The 19th century was characterized by a remarkable outburst of intellectual activity that set in motion radical transformation of India's socio-religious ideas. It was a period when the eight-century-long Islamic domination of Indian political life had come to a decisive end and British rule had planted firm roots. It was also a time when due to several historical factors social and religious thoughts were undergoing profound changes.

Overall, there was confusion and diverse opinions about what 'Hinduism' meant and how indigenous religions—both Vedic and non-Vedic—could be interpreted: at around the same time Western liberal ideas were inspiring new outlook and aspiration. The spirit of rational enquiry had begun to develop in the minds of a section of Indians who began questioning outdated rituals and practices then prevalent in society. The country was swept over by a wave of intellectual unrest and a significant group of educated youth began to feel the need for positive action-oriented social reform. The situation was ripe for the emergence of a religious reform movement resembling the millenarium, which had earlier taken place in other parts of the world.

The spirit of the age was most illustrated by the life and thoughts of Raja Rammohan Roy, considered the steward of this new awakening. In 1814 Rammohan founded the Atmiya Sabha through which he initiated a crusade against social ills. Atmiya Sabha attracted a substantial section of the Bengal aristocracy, including the Tagore family. Rammohan's objective was to awaken the people from their deep slumber and "dream of error" by applying human reason and a rational approach.

During the same time William Adam, a Baptist missionary, converted to the Unitarian Concept of Rammohan Roy and joined hands with him in starting a small Unitarian congregation in Calcutta. In 1828 the works and activities of the Atmiya Sabha were made more broad-based and renamed as Brahmo Sabha. Two years later, it was renamed Brahmo Samaj. The rest, as they say, is history, with the Brahmo Samaj bringing about many far-reaching changes in the country's socio-political ideas and thoughts.

The Brahmo Samaj was a congregation or an order, rather than a sect or community. It sought to strengthen Roy's doctrine of universal brotherhood by making the ideals of love and service towards humanity an essential part of the Brahmo faith. The Samaj stood for the "adoration of the Eternal Unsearchable and Immutable Being who is the author or preserver of the universe". It admitted no image or statue and stood for the promotion of benevolence, charity, morality and virtue. Rammohan conceived it mainly as a common platform for the different religious groups of India.

The Brahmo Samaj was to pass through various stages of evolution during the first four decades of its existence. Under Rammohan the Samaj was characterized by simplicity and catholicity of ideas and this gave Rammohan's successor Maharshi Devendra Nath Tagore the perfect foundation for carrying forward the spirit of the movement. Devendra Nath who joined the Brahmo Samaj in 1843 provided it with solid organizational machinery, his experience as founder of the Tattwabodhini Sabha (1839) (with the aim of disseminating information and correct knowledge of Brahma as defined in the Vedanta and which had been able to attract the cream of the then Bengali intelligentsia, including Ishwar Chandra Vidyasagar, Rajnarayan Bose and Ramtanu Lahiri) helping him immensely.

In the year 1857 Keshab Chandra Sen, then a 20-year-old, joined the Samaj. While Debendranath was a conservative reformist and tried to keep the Samaj free from disruptive foreign influences, Keshab Chandra was imbued with the romantic spirit of liberalism. His radical ideas that included inter-caste marriage, widow remarriage and change in the rites of worship were not encouraged by Devendra Nath and finally in 1866 a split occurred, dividing the Samaj into two factions.

While Devendra Nath remained deeply attached to the Adi Brahmo Samaj, Keshab Chandra with his broad and universal approach started the Bharatbashiya Brahmo Samaj. However, the latter was destined to split again and Keshab Chandra, the great apostle of religious unity, could not prevent it. A large section of his followers disagreed with him on some socio-religious issues and broke away in 1878 under the leadership of Sivanath Sastri. This brought into existence the more democratic Sadharan Brahmo Samaj, which even got the blessings of Debendranath Tagore and Rajnarayan Bose.

It was in the 1860s that the ideas of Brahmo Samaj began to penetrate the north-eastern part of India. Educated youths from Assam were starting to go to Calcutta for higher studies since Calcutta was then the dream destination for intellectual stimulation. During their stay there, these youths, many of whom were to bring far-reaching changes in the intellectual and social life of Assam, were inspired by Rammohan Roy's ideals and Brahmo Samaj activities. Jagnaram Khargaria Phukan, Anadaram Dhekial Phukan, Gunabhiram Baruah, Padmanath Gohain Baruah, Manik Chandra Barua, Lakshminath Bezbaruah, Jagannath Baruah, Kalicharan Mech and others were highly impressed with the Brahmo Samaj's initiative of social reform.

Inspired by the Bengal Renaissance they too began conceiving of a new Assam that could come through socio-cultural change and material progress. This group, the product of a new enlightened age, was the first to think of opening schools for the education of both boys and girls, supporting widow remarriage and opposing polygamy. They submitted memorandums to the government to lighten the tax burden, change the opium policy, increase the number of law courts and give due recognition to the Assamese language.

Besides this group, there were many others who did not go to Calcutta but were nonetheless influenced by Brahmo ideas. Padmahash Goswami, Kamala Kanta Bhattacharyya, Hem Chandra Barua, Braja Sundari Devi, Ananda Ram Goswami, Lakshmikanta Barkataki embraced the Brahmo faith and worked selflessly for a better society.

Complementary efforts were made by many Bengali Brahmo officers, who since 1860 had begun to settle in Assam on the employment of the British Indian government. In their own way this committed group of Brahmos contributed to the cause of education, health and other areas, thereby contributing to the spread of Brahmo ideologies. Social activists and Brahmo emissaries like Nilmani Chakravarty and Avinash Chandra Lahiri rendered yeomen service in the uplift of the tribals of the region.

According to Sivanath Sastri (*The History of Brahmo Samaj*) there were 360 Brahmos in Assam at the beginning of the 20th century (1901).[1] But although microscopic in terms of number, the contribution they made in different fields cannot be underestimated. At a time when the spirit of the so-called Bengal Renaissance had touched Assam and Christian missionary efforts were on to bring about changes in the province, the Brahmo Samaj activists in their own way were able to create a positive socio-cultural impact. They took a lead in education and cultural regeneration in the growing administrative towns of the province—Dhubri, Goalpara, Nagaon, Tezpur, Guwahati and Shillong.

The Brahmo Samaj also played important role in the Khasi and Jaintia Hills during the last quarter of the 19th century and first half of the 20th century. Philanthropic efforts of Brahmo missionary Nilmani Chakravarty and other members of the Brahmo fraternity supplemented Christian missionary efforts to educate the people and bring other societal changes. On occasions they worked in association with the Unitarian church whose members had high regard for Brahmo Samaj. A few Khasi families also embraced Brahmoism and took initiative in establishing schools and rendering humanitarian service. Individuals like Jeeban Roy who was closely associated with Brahmo Samaj activities in Shillong were, in the true sense of the term, torchbearers of change in Khasi society.

Brahmo emissaries from Bengal like Aghorenath Gupta, Ramkumar Vidyaratna and Dwarakanath Ganguly rendered immense service towards the emancipation of the tea garden coolies of Assam, victims of the crudest form of capitalist exploitation under Planter Raj. But for their efforts, the sorry tale of the tea garden workers would have remained untold for a long time.

Sadly, the significant contribution of the Brahmo Samajists has remained a totally neglected field of research in the region. Though much has been researched and written on the contribution made by American and Baptist missionaries in different fields in the region, little has been done to highlight the role of the Brahmo Samaj. Of course Amalendu Guha in his *Planter Raj to Swaraj: Freedom Struggle and Electoral Politics in Assam 1826-1947* did touch upon the subject, as did other pieces of writing like articles by B. Dutta Ray, Gautam Neogi and this author in different volumes of *Proceedings of the North-East India History Association,* K.K. Dasgupta's article on Brahmo Samaj (in S.P. Sen edited *Social and Religious Reform Movements in India*), Rajen Saikia's recently published work *Social and Economic History of Assam 1853-1921* and Tillotama Misra's *Swarnalata*, a novel based on the life of an Assamese Brahmo lady. However, a detailed analysis of the Brahmo movement in the region has remained largely beyond the scope of their studies.

The first hand accounts of coolie exploitation in Assam written by some Brahmo missionaries in the nineteenth century are also available for consultation now. For example, the new edition and reprint of Ramkumar Vidyaratna's *Coolie Kahini* (first published in 1888, Reprints 1982, 1985), *Udasin Satyasrabar Assam Bhraman* (undated, Reprint 1982) and thirteen articles written by Dwarakanath Ganguly, Asst. Secretary of the Indian Association (which has been compiled into a book by Kanailal Chattopadhyaya) give us vivid pictures of the sufferings of the tea garden workers of Assam under the British planters.

Dwarakanath had come to Assam as the Indian Association representative and also as Brahmo Samaj reporter for *Sanjibani* in 1886. His book *Slavery in British Dominion* is an invaluable document for the scholars who are engaged in research on labour history of the region during the colonial period. His reports on different subjects related to the region starting from education, health, labour problem, emigration acts and Brahmo activities were regularly published in the *Brahmo Public Opinion*, *Tattakoumudi Patrika*, *The Indian Messenger*, *Sanjibani* and other Brahmo newspapers and magazines.

Reprints of *Oronodoi* (Maheswar Neog ed.) and some other papers in which articles of contemporary Brahmo Samajists, Brahmo admirers and members of the emerging intelligentsia of Assam (Gunabhiram Barua, Kamalakanta Bhattacharyya, Braja Sundari Devi, Padmabati Devi Phukanani, Hem Chandra Barua, Padmahash Goswami, Ratnakanta Mahanta, Lakshminath Bezbaruah and others) were published also provide important source material for researchers. Articles that appeared in the *Dacca Prakash*, *Bengalee*, *Amrita Bazaar Patrika* also provide good source material for interested scholars in the related field.

Scholars now have access to the original editions of some significant works of the 19th century relating to Assam including *Udasin Satyasrabar Asam Bhraman* (by Ramkumar Bhattacharjee), *Asam Bhraman* (author unknown), *Sudharmar Upakhyan* by Padmabati Debi Phukanani. Two small booklets—*Brahmo Dharmano Kak Bole* (by Padmahash Goswami, 1874), *Brahmo Dharmar Lakhman* (by Padmahash Goswami, 1873) are also available for consultation at the Oriental and India Office collections, London. Different works of Sivanath Sastri, Hem Chandra Barua, Lakshminath Bezbaruah, Kamalakanta Bhattacharyya (Prafulla Dutta Goswami ed) Jnanabhiram Baruah (J.N. Bhuyan ed.) also throw light on different aspects of the Brahmo movement and reflect its concern on issues like polygamy, widow remarriage, status of women, higher education and protection of local and indigenous language. Works of Prasenjit Choudhury, Jogendra Narayan Bhuyan, Amar Dutta and some other contemporary writers help us get a better understanding on the subject.

Biographies and diaries of some eminent Brahmo Samaj members like that of Lakshminath Bezbarauh's *Mor Jiban Sowaran*, Sivanath Sastri's *Atmajibani*, Sarada Manjari Debi's *Mahajatrar Pathe*, Subarna Prabha Das's *Jharapata*, Jnanabhiram Barua's *Mor Katha,* etc., contain a lot of information as do small volumes and booklets like *Mahapran Atul Chandra Roy, Shadhanasramer Itibritta, Bhakta Sadhak Mathura Nath Nandi, Mahapran Ramesh Chandra Mukherjee, Subarna Prabha Das O Tatkalin Nari Samaj, Brahmo Samaj and the Depressed Classes*.

It needs to be mentioned here that not many primary records and papers relating to the history of the Brahmo Samajes of the region are available now. Land grant and trust deeds of different temples have been lost. Except for the Dhubri, Guwahati and Shillong temples, all others have been demolished and temple lands encroached upon. Not much of the above mentioned sources have been utilized or explored by the students of history. No full-length study on the impact of the Brahmo movement in the region has been undertaken so long.

This study, based on hitherto unexplored primary and secondary sources and personal interviews attempts at documentation of these sources. Further, the study based on historical methods of investigation aims to investigate the impact of the Brahmo Samaj movement as well as reassess the contribution of Brahmo emissaries and local Brahmo activists in north-east India. The author has tried to utilize all possible sources and build the narrative thematically in three chapters, thus throwing some light on this lesser explored field of research—with the aim of drawing a more comprehensive picture of the Brahmo Samaj activities and its impact in north-east India.

1

BRAHMO SAMAJ AND THE BRAHMAPUTRA VALLEY

The Brahmo Samaj was going through a very interesting and colourful phase under the leadership of Devendra Nath Tagore and Keshab Chandra Sen when its message reached Assam. A group of Assamese youths who had gone to the neighbouring province of Bengal for higher studies had been initiated into its ideals; and, at around the same time, a group of officials who had come to Assam from Sylhet on government appointments also brought in the message of the Brahmo movement to this far eastern corner of India.

Records reveal that the earliest branches of the Brahmo Samaj in undivided Assam were established in Dhubri, Goalpara, Guwahati, Nagaon, Dibrugarh, Silchar, Shillong and Tezpur between 1868 and 1883, Dhubri and Goalpara being the oldest among them. Sylhet also had a Brahmo Samaj Mandir that was established in 1862. In Jamuguri, Sivasagar, Gauripur, Lumding and Digboi too there were many Brahmo followers, albeit the places did not boast of any Samaj premises.

Jagnaram Khargaria Phukan (1805-38) was the first Assamese gentleman who was attracted to the Brahmo faith. Before becoming the Sadar Amin of Guwahati, Phukan had gone to Calcutta in 1826 where he came into contact with Rammohan Roy. Phukan participated in prayers with the latter and was greatly inspired by Rammohan's teachings. He was perhaps the first Assamese who learnt English by his own efforts. Quoting

Adam White, Amalendu Guha writes that Jagnaram ate and drank freely with the Europeans and procured a variety of wines and European delicacies from Calcutta . . . his house at Guwahati was furnished with chairs, tables, carpets, organs.[1] Phukan's acquaintance with Rammohan helped him develop a progressive mindset and imbued with liberal Brahmo ideas he even wrote letters opposing *satidah* in the *Samachar Darpan*. In the true sense of the term Jagnaram became Rammohan's *fidus attaches,* an early dreamer of bringing change in the region. He was one of the earliest advocates of education and even wished to open schools; but his desire was to remain unfulfilled as he met with an untimely death at the age of 33.

The first Brahmo activist to visit Assam was Maharshi Devendra Nath Tagore in 1849. Debendranath however did not come to preach Brahmo ideals but to avoid being in his ancestral home during the Durga Puja as also to visit the temple of goddess Kamakhya. Then a respected citizen of Bengal, he was honoured with visits of several leading citizens of Assam, including the Commissioner of lower Assam.[2]

The earliest Brahmo missionary who visited the province and toured the Brahmaputra valley in 1870 was Aghorenath Gupta.[3] Aghorenath's preachings enthused many in Nagaon, foremost among whom was Padmahash Goswami (1845-1879), a school teacher from the Jakhalabandha Satra.

Gunabhiram Baruah (1834-94), a highly placed government official also came into contact with Aghorenath. He had been greatly influenced by Brahmo ideals since 1859 when he was stationed at Calcutta, and also assisted Aghorenath arrange his passage, stay and organize meetings with much enthusiasm. Gunabhiram, who hailed from upper Assam was educated in Presidency College at Calcutta. He studied law and even ran a printing press at Calcutta—The Calcutta New Press—along with his cousin Anandaram Baruah. Later, he joined government service in Assam and served in various responsible positions, including that of a first class Magistrate.[4]

During his stay in Calcutta, Gunabhiram attended several Brahmo Samaj meetings and was even present at the first two widow remarriages organized by Ishwar Chandra Vidyasagar in 1856. (The first widow remarriage took place on December 7, 1856 when Srish Chandra Vidyaratna married Jagatkali Debi and the second took place two days later, on December 9.) But it was not until a decade later, in 1869, that he formally embraced Brahmo faith at the Dhubri Brahmo Samaj.[5] It is most likely that Gunabhiram was initiated to the new faith on August 22, the foundation day of the Bharatbashiya Brahmo Samaj. It is known that on that day Sivanath Sastri and a number of youths throughout eastern India were initiated into the Brahmo faith.[6]

Gunabhiram was deeply moved by Ishwar Chandra Vidyasagar's efforts for the uplift of women and started expressing his views on this matter in a series of articles in the *Orunodoi*.[7] Openly advocating the cause of women's education, he wrote that the condition of Assam would never improve if the doors of education were not opened to women. Gunabhiram was also opposed to child marriage, then prevalent both in Assam and Bengal. He was of the opinion that if the age difference between the groom and bride were wide it would be more a father-daughter relationship, causing unhappiness to both.[8] All his articles clearly reflected his concern for widows, the inferior position of women and the need for educating them. Opining that inequality of gender was in contradiction to natural laws, Gunabhiram wrote that God created men and women equals and emphasized that it was an offence to consider men superior to women.[9] Advocating the cause of widow remarriage, the first Assamese to do so, Gunabhiram justified it on the basis of the *sastras,* particularly the *Manusamhita*. He emphasized that no religion prohibited widow remarriage nor were Hindu lawmakers averse to it. He further pointed out that it was already prevalent among different non-Hindus of the Assamese community.[10]

Impressed with the introduction of widow remarriage in Bengal, Gunabhiram in a letter addressed to the editor of *Orunodoi* in December 1856 had even suggested that the year be marked as year of *Bidhaba bibaha* in history.[11] Before him, none in the

Brahmaputra Valley was so vocal on these social issues.[12]

Gunabhiram Baruah's efforts to spread the ideals of the Brahmo faith were intensely supported by Padmahash Goswami, a young gentleman of Nagaon. Born in a distinguished Assamese family, Padmahash was right from his very childhood inquisitive by nature, and as he grew up his faith in the traditional *sastras* began to wane. On a number of occasions he came into confrontation with his gurus on the analysis of the *sastras*—particularly the Vedas and the Upanishads. In 1870 he came to Guwahati for further studies and that very year a Brahmo Samaj was established at Guwahati. Padmahash came into contact with some Brahmo gentlemen of the town and was deeply impressed by the ideology of Brahmo Samaj. On his return to Nagaon he took up teaching in a school. Around that time Brahmo missionary Aghorenath Gupta, who was touring different parts of Assam, visited Nagaon and Padmahash met him several times. Soon he was to embrace Brahmo faith and become quite vocal in preaching its ideals. Other than Gunabhiram Baruah, he was the lone person then to embrace theism.

Padmahash and Gunabhiram's initiation to the Brahmo faith created ripples of discontentment in the then Assamese society. The ripple soon turned into a wave when Gunabhiram, true to his zeal of social reform, married Bishnupriya Devi, a Brahmin widow at Dhubri in 1869. Bishnupriya Devi was the daughter of Lambadar Kakati and was earlier married to Parshuram Barua who died in 1863.[13] This marriage was registered in 1872 after the Native Marriage Act of 1872 came into force, which was passed mainly due to efforts of the Brahmo Samaj under the leadership of Keshab Chandra Sen. Incidentally this was the first registered marriage and possibly the second widow remarriage in Assam.[14] Widow remarriage in traditional Assamese high society of the nineteenth century was not an easy task, but Gunabhiram showed extraordinary courage and sincere commitment of purpose in setting an example.

While Gunabhiram did not have to face ostracism because

of his elevated social position, Padmahash had to face society's wrath head on. The latter created a sensation when on his return to Nagaon from Guwahati, he publicly burnt his sacred thread in the presence of his guru, parents and kinsmen. For this act he was ousted from his home and had to face social boycott for some time. His guardians even wrote to Rajnarayan Basu, the President of Adi Brahmo Samaj challenging the justification of such acts.[15]

However, Padmahash faced the fury with dignity and soon regained public trust through scholastic attainments and philanthropic works. Throughout his life he worked incessantly for the welfare of the community and soon became so influential that "even the Goswamis of Auniati, the powerful center of Brahminical influence of Assam had to look upon him with awe and reverence."[16] His unshakeable faith also attracted a couple of young people to Brahmo ideology. Inspired by his act of throwing away the sacred thread, another Brahmo youth, Ananda Ram Goswami also cast off his holy thread while embracing the Brahmo religion in 1878 and for this act had to face "severe ordeal of persecution."[17]

Sivnath Sastri recorded in the *History of Brahmo Samaj* how Padmahash and Gunabhiram took up the work of Brahmo Samaj in right earnest, as a result of which the Samaj started functioning at Nagaon. Sastri writes: "Nagaon became a source of new influence in Assam in the seventies. From there Brahmoism spread to other centers."[18]

What were the activities of the Brahmo Samaj at Nagaon? Reports in contemporary newspapers of Calcutta provide a glimpse. According to *The Brahmo Public Opinion:* "During the Durga Puja vacation, Babu Gurunath Dutta and Padmahash Goswami preached theism to the people of the district. The secretary distributed gratis about a hundred copies of his pamphlet on Brahmoism. . . . Under the auspices of the Samaj a *prarthana* society has been established at Jamuguri—a village situated at a distance of about seven miles from this town. The establishment of the Samaj owes a great deal to the indefatigable exertions of Baboos Anandaram Goswami and

Kanak Chandra Sarmah. The wife of Baboo Gunabhiram Baruah of Nagaon and Baboo Lakhi Kanta Das paid Rs.60 and Rs.10 respectively for building of the Samaj.... Baboo Sarat Chandra Majumder has let a portion of his *patta* land for the erection of the Samaj building which was removed from its old site."[19]

During prayers at the Nagaon Brahmo Samaj, Gurunath Dutta performed the role of *acharya,* and the threesome—Gunabhiram, Padmahash and Gurunath—conducted regular discourses. *Maghotsava* festival was also held annually, and a good number of participants from the cross section of the society including the Hindus, the Muslims and the Christians participated. And then, it was at the Nagaon Brahmo Samaj that Gunabhiram and Padmahash introduced the *bargeets* of Sankardeva and Madhavdeva in Brahmo prayers.[20]

EARLY BRAHMO MISSIONARIES IN ASSAM

Some Brahmo Missionaries who came to Assam in the nineteenth century left a deep impression among a section of the Assamese society, though it must be admitted that the number of Assamese converts to Brahmo faith were not many. After Devendra Nath Tagore and Aghorenath, Ramkumar Vidyaratna was possibly the third Brahmo emissary who came to Assam. Ramkumar came to the province several times with a dual mission: to preach the Brahmo faith and to acquire first-hand knowledge about the condition of the plantation workers of Assam. He extensively toured Assam, including Sivasagar, Dhubri, Goalpara, Guwahati, Barpeta, Jorhat and Nagaon. Dwarakanath Ganguly, a Brahmo activist and an office bearer of the Indian Association, visited Assam in 1886 to enquire into the effective implementation of the Coolie Emigration Act in Assam. Sivanath Sastri, the head of the Sadharan Brahmo Samaj visited Dhubri, Goalpara, Guwahati, Tezpur, Nagaon, Sivasagar, Dibrugarh and Shillong in July 1886.[21]

Ramkumar Vidyaratna visited Assam several times, possibly three times between 1878 and 1887. During his tour of Assam, Ramkumar spoke on a number of subjects in different gatherings at Barpeta, Dhubri, Nagaon, Tezpur, Biswanath Chariali, Sivasagar and other places. Some of those were reported in the newspapers. On 31 July 1878 he delivered a talk on "Hope and Prospects of India" at the Nagaon school which was attended by 250 persons.[22] "It was very impressive and eloquent and full of instructive matters" stated a report from Nagaon.[23] At Biswanath Chariali Ramkumar delivered speeches on "Ancient Bards of India" and "Religious Revolution created by Sankardeva and Chaitanya".[24] At Tezpur Ramkumar spoke on "Puratan Kabi". At Sivasagar, subject of Ramkumar's speeches were "The crisis of civilization", "Vaisnavite movements in India and Assam" and "Socially deprived mass of India".[25] At Dhubri Ramkumar delivered talks on several subjects like "What is soul and what is God", "Present crisis of religion", "Arya Dharma and Brahmo Dharma" etc.[26] Ramkumar was a prolific speaker and his meetings everywhere were well attended.[27]

Lakshminath Bezbaruah in his autobiography mentioned the positive impact of Ramkumar Vidyaratna's address at the Sivasagar High School. Bezbaruah wrote in his memoirs: "I observed him (Ramkumar Vidyaratna) very carefully because I wanted to become an orator like him. In fact, for a long time after attending his meeting I rehearsed . . . wherever I got an opportunity—on the roads, in the wild and obviously under the shade of a big tree.[28] Bezbaruah has also recorded the strong reaction that Ramkumar's preachings aroused among the orthodox section of Sivasagar's citizens, Bezbaruah's father took the lead in expressing resentement against Ramkumar.[29] Ramkumar however was well received at the Barpeta Satra where he delivered a lecture.[30]

Ramkumar Vidyaratna, Dwarakanath Ganguly and other Brahmo emissaries left a vivid account of the social conditions prevalent then in Assam, particularly in the tea gardens.[31] Ramkumar wrote two Bengali books, *Udasin Satyasrabar Asam Bhraman and Coolie Kahini*—both invaluable documents of labour history of the province. Dwarakanath Ganguly wrote a series of articles in *Sanjibanee, Bengali* and other newspapers of Calcutta on the conditions of labourers in Assam. Mention may also be made of *Asam Bhraman* that was written by an unknown Brahmo missionary and published in 1893 from Calcutta.[32]

It is to be noted that all Brahmo missionaries who visited Assam had high praise for its Sankari Vaisnavite culture. Possibly they could find many similarities between the Brahmo concept of religion and the monotheistic aspect of Sankardev's teachings. A noteworthy aspect highlighted by Ramkumar and the unknown author of *Assam Bhraman* was the comparatively better status of women in Assam in comparison to Bengal.

Interestingly, although a Brahmo Mandir in Guwahati was established in the late sixties of the nineteenth century, it was later closed down due to the "migration of government officers" to Shillong when it was declared the political headquarters. *Brahmo Public Opinion* reported: "We are sorry to hear that the transfer of the seat of government of the province of Assam to Shillong has among its other effects, led to the closing of Brahmo Mandir at Gowhaty for purposes of public worship. With the migration of government officers, Brahmo officers have also migrated and their place of worship lies deserted. . . . We hear there are one or two Brahmo gentlemen still residing at Gowhaty. We have every confidence in our Brahmo friends there and in the power of truth; and earnestly trust an attempt will be made to revive the Brahmo Samaj at Gowhaty and to enlist local sympathy in its support. May God crown all noble efforts with success."[33]

❑ ❑ ❑

Though the Brahmo faith never became a mass movement in Assam, it did attract a fair number of followers. Many of the Brahmo believers of the period were no doubt Bengalis, but a number of Assamese individuals too were attracted to the faith—Anandaram Goswami, Raghunath Bora, Brajanath Bora, Kanak Chandra Sarmah of Nagaon, Lakheswar Kakati of Kaliabor, Ram Durlabh Majumder, Brahmananda Barkataki, Laksmikanta

Barkataki of Tezpur, Laksminath Das of Dibrugarh, Madhukanta Barua, Harekrishna Sarmah, Dr Lakshmi Prova Bora of Shillong and Dharmakanta Barua of Sibsagar were among those. Resourceful persons like Sarat Chandra Majumder and Gurunath Dutta joined the Samaj at Nagaon. Sahityarathi Lakshminath Bezbaruah too was deeply influenced by its activities and followed Brahmo rituals in his house. He embraced Brahmoism just before his marriage, with Debendranath Tagore taking initiative in the matter. Kamalakanta Bhattacharya (1855-1936), better known as Maharshi Kamalakanta for his patriotic writings, was also a Brahmo. Uday Ram Das, a leading medical practitioner, also embraced Brahmo faith, so also his illustrious son Amiya Kumar Das. Assamese intellectuals like Debendranath Bezbaruah, Ghanakanta Goswami, Brahmananda Borkakoti also embraced Brahmoism.[34] William W. Hunter, who compiled the first statistical account of Assam in 1879, mentions "Brahmo Samaj followers" in the districts of Nagaon and Kamrup.[35] According to the Census of India report, 1901, there were 360 Brahmos in Assam during the period 1891-1901.[36]

Lakshmi Prova Bora, the first lady doctor of the entire north-east, was a Brahmo who rendered philanthropic services at Dhubri, Dibrugarh and Shillong. Bora showed exemplary courage when she parted with her husband as he got married for the second time. It was period when a tradition-bound society was not ready to accept a woman who had deserted her husband. She had to go through a lot of trauma, before she proceeded to Calcutta where she came in contact with some Brahmo Samaj members who helped her get a job as teacher at the Brahmo Balika Vidyalaya there. Saving money from her salary, she then proceeded to Cuttack in Orissa to study medicine. With financial assistance provided to her by Kshirode Prasad Roy Chowdhury (Swarnalata Devi's husband) and Tarun Ram Phukan Lakshmi Prabha passed the LMC Examination.

A social activist, she was greatly inspired by the dedicated services of Nilmani Chakravarty, the Brahmo missionary who was working in the Khasi Hill at that time. Lakshmi Prabha also attended the 1919 session of Assam Association at Barpeta and some sessions of the Assam Sahitya Sabha too. When she expired in 1930 the *Tatwa Koumudi Patrika* of Calcutta published a long obituary highlighting her dedicated work for the community, particularly for the weak and downtrodden sections.[37]

CONTRIBUTION OF BRAHMOS TOWARDS LITERATURE AND NEWSPAPERS IN ASSAM

The literary efforts made by the Brahmos in Assam were quite remarkable. Jadunath Chakravarty, an ardent follower of Keshab Chandra Sen, published a Bengali-English weekly—*Assam Mihir*—from Guwahati in 1872. It was printed at the Chidananda Press in Guwahati, owned by Chidananda Chowdhury who hailed from Sundaria village in Barpeta. Chowdhury who had gone to Calcutta for higher education had met Brahmo Samaj members there and become a great Brahmo admirer.[38] Albeit short-lived, an Assamese journal, *Assam Darpan,* was edited by Lakshminath Barkataki of Tezpur in 1873. Barkataki also edited and published two other periodicals—*Chandrodoi* (monthly) and *Assam Bandhav* (fortnightly).[39]

Gunabhiram Baruah was the founder-editor of *Assam Bandhu,* published in the period 1885-86 from 100, Bowbazar Street, Calcutta. The monthly literary magazine attempted to spread "scientific knowledge" and in its inaugural issue declared that it aimed at a movement. It said: "Movement is a pre-condition for development of education . . . in Assam there is no scope of movement. *Assam Bandhu* aims at removing the want of movement . . . this paper will publish articles on literature, science and arts and provide a forum to the writers to express their opinion, both favourable and unfavourable. We are not the representative of any particular class or group of society. Our only effort will be to carry on a movement through which knowledge is spread.[40]

Many budding writers of the period who later became celebrated authors of the "Jonaki Age" of Assamese literature made their debut in this paper.[41] A literary circle thus came into existence whose members included Ratneswar Mahanta, Brahmananda Goswami, Bholanath Das, Padmahash Goswami, Rudra Bardoloi, Dharmeswar Goswami, Baladev Mahanta, Mahananda Bhattacharjee, Balinarayan Bora, Padmabati Debi Phukanani and others.[42]

Incidentally, *Assam Bandhu,* of which 14 issues were published, was the first *masik patrika* or monthly literary magazine of Assam. Contemporary publications like *Orunodoi* (1846-80), *Assam Bilasani* (1871-83) and *Assam News* (1882-85) claimed to be *sambadpatra* or newspapers.

Deeply inspired by *Bharat Sramajeevi* (the newspaper edited by Sasipada Banerjee of Calcutta which dealt with the problem of the working class people of India), Dharmakanta Barua of Lakhipur (who later settled at Dibrugarh) also brought out a newspaper titled *Digvijay* that highlighted the problems of the common people, including the tea garden labourers of Assam. This paper was published from Dibrugarh.[43] Padmahash Goswami too brought out a periodical named *Gyanodoi* in 1875-76. *Gyanodoi* needs special mention as quite surprisingly this paper failed to get its rightful place in the history of journalism in the province.[44] The paper however has been mentioned in government reports and records of the province of Assam for the year 1874-75 and 1875-76.[45] According to the report of T.B. Mitchell the then Deputy Commissioner of Nagaon, "The *Gyanodoi,* a vernacular publication of about the size of two sheets of letter paper professing to treat of science and literature is published at Calcutta by a native of this district." That this "native" was none other than Padmahash Goswami is evident from a correspondence of the district administration. Subsequent to a controversy that arose regarding the publication of the periodical (since Padmahash was unaware of government rules and had not taken permission of the government before the publication of the paper), A.N. Philips who succeeded Mitchell wrote to the Inspector of Schools defending Padmahash vide his letter No. 195 dated Nagaon June 9, 1876: "Sir with reference to your letter No. 701 dated 2 instant I have the honour to inform you that the manager of *Gyanodoi* periodical Padma Hans Goswami and the Pandit of the Zilla School are one and the same person. He has never it seems obtained the Chief Commissioner's sanction in his conducting this periodical and he has been informed that he was wrong in undertaking the management of it without such sanction. He says the omission was due to ignorance on his part and he now solicits the chief commissioner's sanction. As the paper is a very harmless one and devoted exclusive to scientific and literary subjects I would beg to recommend his application."[46]

In order to promote Brahmo faith among the people of Assam, Padmahash Goswami also published two booklets in Assamese, titled *Brahmo Dharmar Lakkhan* (Features of Brahmo Dharma) and *Brahmo Dharma Kakno Bole* (What is Brahma Dharma).[47] In 1872 he also published *Padmamala,* a collection of twenty-two poems. It was the first compilation of poetry in Assamese language. Another book authored by Padmahash Goswami, *Asamiya Larar Sikhshasar,* was a very popular textbook for school students in Assam during the last quarter of the nineteenth century.[48]

The Times of Assam, the first weekly English newspaper of Assam was published from Dibrugarh on January 5, 1895. Its founder-editor was Radhanath Changkakati (1853-1923) who also edited a monthly magazine called *Asamiya* for some time. He received unqualified support from Basambad Mitra (1858-1948), an advocate who not only wrote editorials for the paper but also became its part and parcel. It was because of Mitra that *The Times of Assam* did not close down immediately after Changkakati's death. Interestingly, both Changkakati and Mitra were great Brahmo Samaj admirers. "He (Changkakati) moulded himself and shaped his family on the lines of the Brahmo Samaj."[49] When the district administration did not allow the Chatra Samaj, a newly-formed students organization, to hold its meeting in any school premise due to political considerations, Changkakati and Mitra arranged the meeting in the premises of the Dibrugarh Brahmo Samaj. While thanking the Brahma Samaj authorities for allowing them to hold the meeting, Changkakati said in his address, "If the knowledgeable section of society lack sympathy for us there are others who come forward to share the load for a good cause—it should be understood that no organization can be ruined even if a section of the society does not cooperate."[50] Radhanath Changkakati's closeness with the Brahmo Samaj also becomes evident when we note that the news of his election as secretary of the first session of the Assam Conference held at Tezpur in 1887 was given much prominence in *The Indian Messenger* in its December 11, 1887 issue.

Then there was the *Assam Hitoishi Patrika*, edited jointly by Kamalakanta Bhattacharya and Mahadev Sarmah, priced at 2 annas per issue (3 annas with postage).[51] It was published between 1925-28 from Calcutta by Kumardev Mukhopadhaya. Kamalakanta, a devoted Brahmo and staunch nationalist, apart from contributing regularly to *Banhi*, *Chetana* and *Jonaki* also introduced a new trend in Assamese writing by publishing thought-provoking articles like *Gutidiyek Chintar Dhou* and *Astabarkar Atmajibani*. He also wrote a book *Koh Pantha* that is considered by many as a pioneering work in modern Assamese literature.

In his writings Kamalakanta attacked the prevalent caste system and openly criticized the parasitic qualities of the Brahmin priests. This made him very unpopular, and so although he was the most spirited Assamese nationalist-poet of his period, he was not accepted well by contemporary society. It was because he married a widow, gave up the sacred thread and used to consume beef publicly.[52] "His criticism of some aspects of Hinduism, more particularly the dominance of Brahmins in society, made him unpopular. The eccentric iconoclast had torn off his sacred thread, taken to the plough, converted the *saligram* (an idolized stone) into a paper-weight and declared his faith in Brahmoism. The immobility of society made him impatient and the Brahmo faith made him a rebel.

So he could hardly gain the ear of his people. His later life was a tale of misery of every form."[53] He was not only excommunicated from the society, a systematic campaign was carried out to defame him. Letters from the orthodox section of the society started appearing against Kamalakanta in Brahmo Newspapers of Calcutta. A letter writer commented on one of Kamalakanta's article: "I am afraid that eccentric man Kamala Kant's contribution which was published in the last issue will create an undesirable sensation among the Gossains against whom he has thundered froth a bitter anathema. There is no solidarity in it, it is pure a dilettantism. I must say the man is a pretender. He pretends to be a reformer, or a patriot, neither of which he can be. His utterances are something like the ravings of a cracked brain ... I am sure big and learned Gossains like ours will pass over it as a contentious piece unworthy of taking notice of."[54]

Gunabhiram Baruah as founder-editor of *Assam Bandhu,* published during 1885-86, aimed to spread "scientific knowledge". Among his many literary works, mention may be made of *Ram Navami* (drama), *Anandaram Dhekial Phukanar Jivan Charita, Assam Buranji, Lora Punthi* and editing Anandaram Dhekial Phukan's *Asamia Lorar Mitra. Ram Navami,* depicting the fate of the Brahmin widows in society and written in a satirical form, acted as a whip on the prevailing social system. It was the first full-length Assamese social drama and has immense literary value. Tilottama Misra comments: "The play itself, though artistically of a rudimentary nature, contains several points of historical and literary interest. From the literary point of view, it was the first Assamese social tragedy written under the influence of the English tragic drama, tragedy as a form being unknown to earlier Assamese drama. Thus, in the true spirit of Renaissance, Gunabhiram borrowed freely from a variety of sources and tried to reshape this material in the light of his individual sensibility."[55]

Lakshmikanta Barkakati edited a monthly magazine titled *"Chandradoi"*. He also edited a weekly Newspaper, *Assam Bandhav* and both these papers made significant contribution towards journalism in Assam. Both papers publishered news and articles on contemporary social issues.

Maheswar Barua the second editor of the Assamese daily *Sadiniya Asamiya* (the paper was owned by Chandra Kumar Agarwalla), was a Brahmo. Barua successfully edited the paper for few years since 1922.

It is worth mentioning that till the 2nd decade of the twentieth century the Brahmo Public Opinion and the Indian Messenger had good circulation in Assam. For example 139 copies of Brahmo Public Opinion was sold in different places of Brahmaputra Valley (Dhubri, Guwahati, Goalpara etc.) in 1894. In the same year Shillong had 42 subscriptions of the Newspaper.[56]

Gunabhiram Baruah's wife Bishnupriya Devi, also authored two Assamese books—*Sadhukathar Punthi* and *Nitikatha*, have always been considered important early literary efforts by an Assamese lady.[57] These two books were unique because Bishnupriya Devi collected the tales from different ethnic sources and were written at the nascent stage of Assamese children's literature.[58]

Lakshminath Bezbaruah's wife Pragnasundari Devi (the granddaughter of Maharshi Debendranath Tagore) was the first to write an Assamese cookery book—*Randha-bora.*[59] She also wrote *Amish o Niramish Ahar* in Bengali in three volumes.

These publications were important contributions to Assamese journalism and literature, next only to the *Orunodoi* phase and contemporary *Jonaki* age. The contribution of Lakshminath Bezbaruah does not have to be emphasized: he was in the true sense the doyen of modern Assamese literature. Apart from writing a number of poems, novels, short stories, dramas, biographies and numerous articles, Bezbaruah also authored *Bharatbarshar Buranji* and *The Religion of Love and Devotion*. He edited a few volumes of *Jonaki* and was the founder-editor of *Banhi.* Right from his student days and more particularly after his marriage to Pragnasundari, Bezbaruah came in close contact with Brahmo Samaj officials and this had a definite influence in shaping his vision. He advocated that the educated group of Hindus should extend their hand to cleanse Hinduism of all dirt accumulated over the centuries.[60]

BRAHMOS AND THE INTER COMMUNITY MARRIAGE

Another important development that took place in Assam during the period under the influence of the Brahmos was the introduction of inter-community and inter-caste marriages. Families who had embraced Brahmoism had but limited matrimonial choice and this indirectly led to a better social understanding between the Assamese and other communities. Lakshminath Bezbaruah got married to Pragnasundari Devi of the Tagore family and Anando Ram Goswami, a Brahmo from Nagaon, got married to Ambika Sundari Devi, daughter of a Christian convert Rudra Ram Deka. The marriage that took place on March 26, 1879, at the Nagaon Brahmo Samaj was reported in Brahmo papers in Calcutta.[61] Gurunath Dutta, headmaster of Nagaon Government School also gave his daughter in marriage to Lakshmikanta Barkakati of Tezpur. Dharmakanta Kalita got married to Laksmipriya Sarmah, a Brahmin widow at Nagaon.[62] This marriage, which was performed in accordance with Brahmo rituals at the residence of the headmistress of the local school, Charusila Sen generated much excitement.

Sometimes inter-caste or inter-community marriages between Brahmos drew social attention. The diary of an old gentleman kept in the possession of Santimoy Dasgupta of Dhubri gives an interesting account of a Brahmo marriage in 1894 at the Dhubri Brahmo Mandir where "*baro-saheb, memsaheb* and *hakimsaheb*" were present.[63] As secretary of Nagaon Brahmo Samaj, Padmahash Goswami also reported cases where Europeans and members of Hindu, Christian and Muslim communities were present during Brahmo marriages at Nagaon.[64] The first registered marriage at Tezpur under the New Marriage Act (Act III) of 1872 was held in 1884 where the Deputy Commissioner along with his wife and many European tea estate officials were present. *The Indian Messenger* reports: "A Brahmo marriage according to Act III of 1872 took place on the 29th June in Tezpur, Assam. The bridegroom is Baboo Hridayram Das, bachelor aged 30 years, and the bride is Srimati Sarala Das, the daughter of our friend Lakhsmi Kanta Das aged 15 years, a spinster. Babu Hridayram Das is a native doctor in the tea garden in the district of Nagaon. The marriage was celebrated in the presence of the Deputy Commissioner and his wife and a few more Europeans, and all the educated and Assamese gentlemen of the station. Our missionary brother Pandit Ramkumar Vidyaratna conducted divine service on the occasion."[65] One of the daughters of Maheswar Baruah, the second editor of *Sadiniya Asamiya,* got married to a Christian gentleman. Baruah was a Brahmo and all other marriages in the family were performed as per Brahmo rituals.

It is interesting to note that Gunabhiram Baruah's daughter Swarnalata's marriage to Rabindranath Tagore had also been almost finalized. However, it fell through at the last moment when Maharshi Devendra Nath Tagore learnt that the bride's father had married a widow. Jnanabhiram Baruah, Swarnalata's brother, writes in his memoirs: "Kabiguru's marriage was almost settled with my sister Swarnalata. But when the Maharshi (Devendra Nath Tagore) came to know about it, he disapproved of it and did not allow it to materialize."[66] A beautiful account of the developments relating to the Swarnalata-Rabindranath matrimonial negotiations has been narrated in Tilottama Misra's prize-winning novel *Swarnalata.*

Swarnalata Devi got married twice. Her first marriage was to Dr Nanda Kumar Roy of Calcutta, on whose untimely demise she got married for the second time to Kshirode Chandra Roy Chowdhury, the celebrated littérateur of Bengal who was also the Principal of Hoogly College. Later in 1906, Swarnalata's brother Jnanabhiram Baruah got married to Lotika Devi, the great granddaughter of Debendranath Tagore. "By the standard of the age it was an uncommon marriage relation and it serves as an index of social metamorphosis," writes Rajen Saikia.[67]

EDUCATION IN ASSAM AND THE CONTRIBUTION OF BRAHMOS

The Brahmos took up the cause of education in right earnest. The girls' school at Dhubri started at their initiative. Jagnaram Khargharia Phukan, the first and possibly the only Assamese to come in contact with Raja Rammohan Roy in the 1820s, took initiative to open two schools at Guwahati—one in English medium and the other in Bengali medium. Some Brahmo teachers who dedicated their lives to liberate the minds of the students of Assam from age-old superstitions include Ambika Charan Mukherjee, Padmahash Goswami, Lakhsminath Das, Charushila Devi, Gurunath Dutta, Sarada Manhari Dutta, Subarna Prava Das, Susama Roy, Haliman Dkhar, Kailash Chandra Sen, *et al*.

Ambika Charan Mukherjee rendered yeomen service towards the cause of education at Dhubri where he taught at the girls' school. Some of his students also received government scholarships. His simplicity, fatherly affection and dedicated life encouraged parents to send their daughters to school in large numbers during the 1880s.[68] This might be the reason why the number of girl students in Dhubri was proportionately higher than those in Guwahati during 1880-1900.[69]

The members of Brahmo Samaj were instrumental in opening two more primary schools—one at Silchar and the other at Guwahati. Though the Silchar school was closed down during 1940s, the school at Guwahati continued till 1970s. Banalata Halder served as the first mistress of the Guwahati Brahmo Samaj School. One interesting feature of this school was that the school served the need of the downtrodden section of the society—many of its students were the wards of railway coolies and nearby slum dwellers.

As Headmaster of the Nagaon Government School, Gurunath Dutta also left a mark as did Charushila Sen, the Headmistress of Nagaon Bengali Girls' School.[70] Padmahash Goswami, the Sanskrit teacher of Nagaon Zilla School, wrote articles in the Bengali monthly magazine *Samadarshi,* which was edited by Sivanath Sastri and published from Calcutta. Laksminath Das taught at Dibrugarh School where his simplicity and religious commitment touched everyone. Kailash Nath Sen too became a very reputed teacher at the Guwahati Balika Bidyalaya. Rammohan Balak Vidyalaya, which was established at Dhubri a century ago, is still functioning.[71] A number of gentlemen and women belonging to Brahmo faith served as teachers, Head masters and Head mistress in places like Silchar, Tezpur, Shillong, Dhubri, etc. Satish Chandra Roy, the fourth principal of Cotton College (during 1937-1940) was a Brahmo. He and his wife (a British lady of Christian faith) left a very positive impact on the mind of the youth of Guwahati. Roy also regularly participated in conducting Upasana at Brahmo Samaj, Guwahati. The contribution of Sarada Manjari Dutta, Hemanta Kumari Devi, Sabarna Prava Das, Nilamani Chakravarty, Atulananda Das, Brajo Sundar Roy, Haliman Dkhar, Susama Roy and others to the cause of education in the Khasi Hills were also immense and will be discussed in a separate chapter.

PIONEERING EFFORTS OF THE BRAHMOS IN ASSAM

In their zeal for reform the Brahmo Samaj members, although small in number, became pioneers in different fields. Gunabhiram Baruah's daughter Swarnalata Baruah was the first Assamese lady to go outside the province for higher studies. She studied at Bethune College, Calcutta and also authored the book *Arhi Tirota*. The book depicts the qualities needed to become an ideal lady in society and how to derive satisfaction in life. *Arhi Tirota* is considered an important contribution to Assamese literature. She also wrote some trendsetting articles in *Assam Bandhu* and *Jonaki*.[72] Swarnalata was possibly the first Assamese lady to use a pen name "Hemlata Devi" to publish some of her articles in *Jonaki*.[73] Hemo Bora writes: "Swarnalata was the main woman writer of the *Jonaki* age. In Swarnalata's writings the mentality of the Assamese women of the age have been reflected. Her articles have a distinguished place in the new trend of Assamese prose writing."[74] In fact, Swarnalata was the symbol of a spirit of the new age and greatly admired.

Lakshmi Prabha Bora was the first Assamese lady to go to Cuttack for medical studies and possibly also the first Assamese lady to take up service outside Assam. Before going to Orissa she served at the Brahmo Balika Vidyalaya at Calcutta.[75]

Gunabhiram's son, Karunabhiram Baruah, was the founder-editor of *Lora Bandhu*, the first Assamese children's magazine.[76] Though Karunabhiram died at an early age, he contributed articles in *Assam Bandhu*.[77] Gunabhiram was instrumental in the formation of Gyan Sabha, which aimed at channelising the creative potential of the youth in a positive direction.

Brahmananda Barkakati of Tezpur was a devoted Brahmo. He was closely involved in the activities of Tezpur Brahmo Samaj. Some of his extended family members were deeply influenced by the Brahmo ideologies and imbued with its liberal spirits, made important contributions in different fields Ramakanta Barkakati graduated in Arts and Law from Calcutta in 1880s and served as the first Assamese translator of the Calcutta High Court. Along with some of his friends he translated Shakespeare's *Comedy of Errors* in Assamese. This translated drama, *Bhramaranga,* was also successfully staged at Calcutta.[78] Ramakanta's two daughters, Sudhalata and Sukhalata need special mention because of their unique scholastic attainments. Both had very close connection with the Brahmo elites of Calcutta and they attended Brahmo Samaj prayers regularly. They also changed their surname from Barkakati to "Duarah" which was a rare instance in the then contemporary Assamese society.

Sudhalata, a student of Bethune School, had the distinction of being the first Assamese lady (and possibly the only) to become the topper among the girls who appeared in the Matriculation Examination under Calcutta University in 1914. She graduated from the Bethune College with Honours in

Sanskrit. She created a record in Calcutta University—a record which remains unbroken till now, when she became first class first in M.A. in 1921 obtaining highest marks in seven out of eight papers. She was awarded with eight medals, including gold medals by Calcutta University, for this unique achievement. Later she obtained BT Degree from the same University in 1923. After teaching Sanskrit, and English for a few years, Sudhalata Duarah became the Principal of Cross White College, Allahabad in 1925. She was not only the first lady of Assam to become a graduate, she also was the first Assamese to obtain M.A., B.T. degrees with highest distinction.[79]

Sudhalata's younger sister Sukhalata Duarah also studied with her sister in the same college in the same class. She also obtained her graduation and post-graduation degrees in 1918 and 1921 along with Sudhalata. Securing first division in M.A. she opted for a teaching career. She served at Cross White College and also in a college at Lahore. Later she also became the Principal of a College at Lahore. Sudhalata and Sukhalata's another sister Santilata also passed M.A. and taught at Theosophical College, Beneras and Lady Irwin College, Delhi. After serving for seventeen long years as the Principal of the Delhi College, Santilata became a saint at the later stage of her life and took the name of Swami Santananda and established a hermitage at Bangalore.[80]

Maheshwar Baruah, the second editor of the Sadiniya Asamiya, was much influenced by Gunabhiram Baruah and Lakhsminath Bezbaruah and wanted to go to Calcutta for higher education. His father Mohan Barua (the Sadar Amin of Dibrugarh), however, refused to allow him to go to Calcutta as he felt that like Gunabhiram, his son would also become a Brahmo. Maheshwar became totally frustrated and exhibited his anguish by tearing out and throwing the sacred thread that he was wearing in presence of his father. Later, he embraced the Brahmo faith.[81]

Maheshwar Baruah is not much known in Assam today but his was an interesting and dedicated life. He used to write regularly in the *Times of Assam* and published Assamese translation of different chapters of *Hitopodesh* for which he received warm appreciation from persons like Gnanadabhiram Baruah and Rajani Kanta Bardoloi. Making a comparative study of Sanskrit, Latin and Persian grammar, he prepared an important manuscript, *Dhatukosh*, in Asamese but could not print it as no publisher was then interested to publish the same. He also authored a book titled *"Elementary Grammar and Composition"*. He imparted liberal education to his children and succeeded in sowing the seeds of patriotism in their mind.[82] His second daughter, who served as a school teacher, received stricture from the Government for getting involved in the national movement. His another daughter, despite resentment and opposition from her near and dear ones became a nurse. Maheshwar's daughters were given marriage as per Brahmo marriage rituals. (In one of his daughter's marriage, Kamalakanta Bhattacharya took the lead role which was attended by Chandrakumar Agarwalla, Radhanath Changkakati, Faiznur Ali, Mr. Smith, and Father Joseph.)[83] One of his daughter also got married to a Christian gentleman. Punyaprabha Barua, the youngest daughter of Maheshwar Baruah served as a very successful teacher at Jorhat, Guwahati Government schools and also at Victoria School, Dibrugarh for a long time.[84]

The independent mindset of Maheshwar Baruah was reflected when he published a news item involving the misdeeds of one Mr. Kellvert, the Asst. Superintendent of Police. During the time of the Non co-operation movement, this Kellvert ransacked the *Namghar* (place of religious congregation) of Sundardiya, assuming that the place has become a centre for extremist activities. Not only that, Kellvert publicly urinated at the Namghar which strongly hurt the sentiments of the local people. Gandhiji reported the whole incident in *Young India*. Maheshwar got the entire report from *Young India* translated into Assamese and published that in *Sadiniya Asamiya* in February, 1922. Kellvert filed a defamation case against the newspaper.[85]

Barua fought this case with strong determination with the

spirited support of Chandra Kumar Agarwala, the owner of *Sadinya Asamiya*. Agarwalla engaged Akhil Chandra Dutta, a leading lawyer of *Coomillah* in defense of his case. The case generated much interest in contemporary Assam as this was the first defamation case against a newspaper in Assam and a leading intellectual of the time owned it. Kellvert filed the case against Maheswar Barua and Tulsi Gogoi—the editor and the printer of the paper respectively. The best efforts of Akhil Chandra Dutta did not bear any fruit. A.H.W. Bentinck (the Deputy Commissioner of Guwahati, in whose court the case was filed) in his judgement found Maheswar Barua and Tulsi Gogoi guilty under IPC. Sec 500. He slapped a fine of Rupees one thousand on Barua while Gogoi was fined Rupees One hundred and fifty only. Further the judgement categorically stated that out of the fine levied, Rupees five hundred should be paid to Kellvert.[86] It was interesting to note that while the court proceedings were going on, *Sadiniya Asamiya* published the entire proceedings of the case part by part and thereby tacitly informed the public of Assam how the local paper has been subjected to unprecedented harassment for publishing a news item concerning the *satra* and how the British judge failed to honour the sentiment of the local people in order to protect its erring official on duty.[87]

Barua did his best to serve Assam throughout his life but unfortunately the newspaper of the contemporary conservative society kept a distance from him. His brother severed all relations with him. So were some of the leading citizens of the town. It is not surprising therefore that when he expired the family members had to wait for hours with the dead body as there were not sufficient people from the family relatives to carry the dead body to the crematorium. However some other admirers of Barua including some tribals and persons belonging to Mohemedan faith came forward and took the body to the crematorium.[88]

Most Brahmo followers were no doubt social activists, but some did get actively associated with the nationalist movement. The close association of a number of Brahmo Samajists in the formation of the Indian Association at Calcutta gave the Brahmos a boost. In Assam Kamalakanta Bhattacharya participated in the *swadeshi* movement in 1905-06. He also participated in the first Calcutta session of the Indian National Congress and wrote a number of patriotic poems.

Lakshminath Bezbaruah attended the 1892 Allahabad session of Indian National Congress. Later, as a representative of the Jorhat Sarvajanik Sabha he attended the All India Congress sessions at Madras (1903) and Bombay (1904).

Lakshmi Kanta Barkataki was the key person to start the *Tezpur Ryot Sabha* that aimed to protect the tenants and peasants from enhancement of land revenue by the British government. The *Ryot Sabha* could succeed in spreading nationalist sentiment and establishing a wide base in the rural areas. Its branches were established in a number of villages of Darrang district. With small donations collected from hundreds of peasants, Lakshmi Kanta also built the Tezpur Town Hall in 1887—the first of its kind in Assam. He also attended the sessions of the Indian National Congress at Bombay in 1885 and at Madras in 1887.[89] The *Ryot Sabha* taught people to give expression to their opinion and kept close liaison with the office bearers of the Indian Association in Calcutta, most of whom were Brahmos. The Indian Association at that time earnestly took up the cause of the tea plantation workers of Assam and tried to mobilize public opinion in their favour. Lakshmi Kanta was one of the very few Assamese gentlemen who was associated with the Indian National Movement since its inception. Amiya Kumar Das joined the non co-operation movement of Gandhi leaving his studies at Calcutta Law College in 1921. He also became the President of the Assam Chatra Sanmelan in 1930. He was imprisoned several times during the national movement. Later he was elected to the Assam Legislative Assembly.

Some Brahmo littérateurs made conscious and honest effort to revive Assam's past glory and thereby contributed towards the idea of formation of a composite Assamese nationality during the later part of the nineteenth and early twentieth century. In this process language played an important role. Udayan Misra correctly observes that due to a number of historical factors the idea of Assamese identity was then shifting from "multilingual uniculture" to "unilingual multiculture" during the period.[90] In this process of formation of Assamese national identity, some Assamese Brahmos played a significant role. Kamalakanta Bhattacharyya who participated actively in the national movement in 1905-06, emphasized the protection of the distinct identity of the Assamese people. In his writings Kamalakanta spoke of Assam's past glory and said that economic advancement was the key to its progress. Lakshminath Bezbaruah, on the other hand, emphasized on the cultural resurgence of the Assamese people that could be brought about by reinvigorating the Assamese language. In the true spirit of Brahmo rationality, Bezbaruah never failed to recognize the role of other religions, particularly the Vaisnavite movement, as the cementing factor in the melting-pot culture of Assam. He wrote: "Assam and the Assamese people are the product of assimilation of many nationalities, people and languages. . . . In Assam there remained a cementing force that is not found in other regions. This cementing force is the satra institutions that are instrumental in popularizing the Vaisnavite faith. The nucleus of the Assamese language can be found in Sanskrit . . . Sanskrit has the status of mother language of the Assamese."[91]

According to Misra "two types of nationalism co-existed side by side."[92] This was, however, a common phenomenon throughout India at that point of time. Many a time a section of the local intelligentsia were instrumental in reviving past glory of their respective regions considering that regional consciousness was a precondition to nascent and emerging idea of broader nationalism.[93] If Rabindranath Tagore wrote *Amar Sonar Bangla, ami tomai bhalobashi,* Lakshminath Bezbaruah wrote *O mor aponar desh*.

❑ ❑ ❑

In other fields also, Brahmos, though microscopic in terms of number, made significant contribution. Gunabhiram Baruah about whom we have discussed earlier, was a high-ranking Assamese officer of the Government of Eastern Bengal and Assam of those days who rose to the position of first class executive magistrate. He was among the minuscule group of British government officials of eastern Bengal and Assam who was awarded the title Rai Bahadur in 1887 (while still in service) for administrative efficiency. When Gunabhiram Baruah went on superannuation in 1890, the Chief Commissioner of Assam Valley recognized his services to the government in the following words: "The Chief Commissioner cannot allow the occasion of the retirement of Rai Gunabhi Ram Sarmah Baruah Bahadur, the senior extra assistant commissioner in this province, to pass by without recording his sense of very valuable services rendered to the government by that officer throughout an extended period. These services have been in every way deserving of public recognition which is hereby accorded to them."[94] Gunabhiram got his rightful place in the socio-literary history of Assam. But there were also other Brahmo officers holding comparatively lower ranks in the administrative hierarchy of the province who earned enviable compliments. Ramesh Chandra Mukherjee, head assistant of Dhubri Deputy Commissioner's office, is a case in point. Towards the end of the nineteenth century and early twentieth century Mukherjee became an important figure in British official circles in Goalpara and the local community because of his honesty and integrity. Sir Arthur Coming, who served as Deputy Commissioner before joining as the Judge of the Calcutta High Court commented that Ramesh Chandra was "scrupulously honest". Mc Blen, another Deputy Commissioner under whom Ramesh Chandra served, commented: "Babu R.C. Mukherjee, a member of the Brahmo Samaj, is a gentleman for whom I have a great regard. He is a refreshing contrast as regards morals to many of the persons who hold or held good position in Dhubri."[95] On another occasion Mc Blen said, "Oh, Brahmo Samajists? They are very respectable people!"[96]

So, even though Ramesh Chandra served in a comparatively

lower position in the administrative hierarchy, because of his honesty and integrity the government appointed him supervisor of the Bijni Raj estate with additional responsibility to impart moral and general education to the minor king of the same estate. These are pointers to the fact that the microscopic group of Brahmo Samajists in Assam could leave a mark and earn respectable positions. Gunabhiram's and Ramesh Chandra's are but just two instances.

BRAHMO SAMAJ ACTIVITIES: RIPPLES IN THE SOCIETY

In their zeal for reform, some youths took up novel methods to bring radical changes in society. No doubt they were inspired by the work of the Brahmo Samajists but their methods of preaching were quite peculiar. We get an interesting account of these youth missionaries in the writings of Brahmo missionary Nilmani Chakravarty. In 1889, on his way from Calcutta to Shillong, Nilmani stayed at the Guwahati residence of a Brahmo gentleman, Nishi Kanta Ghosh, for a few days. During this time he met two youths, Akbar Mukunda Godson and Akbar Jogindra Godson (son of God), who were in Guwahati distributing books and magazines. The two had done away with their original names and taken on new names in order to remove the influence of caste system and to spread the message of universal brotherhood. In order to practice austerity and show concern for animals, they had also become strict vegetarians. One of their friends by the name Vinod Ladies Friend (Friend of women) also began preaching the message of women's emancipation in upper Assam, all the while claiming to be a Brahmo. Even though these youths were courteous, people were annoyed with them because of their peculiar names, dress and lifestyle.

Nilmani wrote that when he met the sub-deputy collecter of Guwahati Babu Chandra Kanta Sen, a Brahmo sympathizer, Sen told him that the Sadharan Brahmo Samaj had been wrong in sending these people for missionary work—an allegation that Nilmani denied.[97] But this interesting episode clearly showed how Brahmo Samaj activities had inspired some youth to take up social reform activities.

❑ ❑ ❑

While discussing the impact of Brahmo Samaj movement it will not be out of context to refer to a monotheistic religion that spread among the Bodos in Assam at the beginning of the twentieth century. It was a time when parallel monotheist movements, free from idolatry and superstition, were taking place in other parts of India. The *Paramhansa Sabha* in Maharashtra for example was established in 1849. (It later became *Prarthana Samaj* under the leadership of Dr. Atmaram Panduranga.) *Hitakari Samajam* of Veersalingam Pantulu Kandukuri of Andhra Pradesh was another that had a distinct Brahmo influence.

Among the Bodos a similar movement, known as '*Brahma Dharma*' spread in the late nineteenth century. The protagonists of this faith ascribe its origin to one Paramhansa Sibnarayan Swami who hailed from the West.[98] However, it was Kalicharan Mech (who later changed his surname from Mech to Brahma) of Kazigaon, Goalpara who was really responsible for propagating and popularizing the faith among the Bodos. The religion attracted a good number of followers in lower Assam and some areas of North Bengal. Though this group believed that only Brahma is the supreme God to whom *ahuti* can be offered, its other principles and activities had striking similarity with the Brahmo Samaj movement. For example, Kalicharan called upon the Bodo people to do away with host of deities and sacrifices of fowl, pigeon, etc. He gave a clarion call to the people to give up traditional practices of rearing pigs and poultry in unhygienic conditions and made an appeal to the village community to give up the habit of drinking liquor. Kalicharan discredited the practice of bride price then prevalent in Bodo society and encouraged the establishment of the first Mahila Samity. He was also responsible for organizing the first Bodo Mahasanmelan. Championing the cause of self-employment and importance of entrepreneurship, he established carpentry and weaving centers for providing jobs to youths. He named the religion Brahma Dharma and petitioned to the Deputy Commissioner to allow them to use the title of "Brahma". A.G. Lainy, the then Deputy Commissioner of Goalpara granted the permission. Since then the title Brahma began to be used by the Bodo community. The striking similarity between Kalicharan's faith and the Brahmo Samaj prompts us to think whether the original preacher of the religion was in any way influenced by Brahmo Samaj ideals. This becomes all the more pertinent when we learn that both Kalicharan and Sibnarayan Swami had stayed at Calcutta in the nineteenth century for quite sometime.[99]

The ideals and principles of the Brahmo movement convinced many leading Assamese gentlemen of the nineteenth century though they did not formally convert into the Brahmo faith. Jaduram Deka Barua who served as munsif of Jorhat and later became the *Sadar Amin* of Barpeta openly supported Brahmo activities through his writings in *Samachar Darpan*, Calcutta. He publicly denounced evil practices like satidaha and human sacrifice and tried to mobilize public opinion towards its abolition. Not only did he support widow remarriage, he also set an example by marrying a widow. This marriage was incidentally the first widow remarriage in Assam.

It is worth mentioning that Hem Chandra Barua (1835-1896), Gunabhiram Barua and Kamalakanta Bhattacharyya were the first three social revolutionaries of modern Assam. Though a Brahmin by birth, Assam's great litterateur, writer (author and publisher of Assamese dictionary, *Hemkosh*) and social reformer Hem Chandra Barua engaged *Sudra* cooks in his house. Not only that, he kept his cooks well dressed and purchased watches for them which amounted to social revolution in those days.[100] A true rationalist and an agnostic, Baruah understood the importance of women's education for the upliftment of the society and wrote several articles on the subject. He was much influenced by the Brahmo movement and the contemporary Bengal renaissance, though like Gunabhiram, he did not pursue his education at Calcutta. With simple arguments he supported Widow Remarriage and wrote in his autobiography: "I support widow remarriage; but I just do not suggest that a lady should be given marriage again if she becomes a widow. But in my view, the obstacle that stands in the path of widow remarriage should be removed. If that is done, then a widow might get married just like a widower gets married after the death of his wife. Those who are widowed at childhood or before the birth of a child, their marriage is a necessity".[101]

Baruah also wrote letters to Orunodoi protesting polygamy and also strongly criticized the habit of consumption of opium by the people of Assam.[102] Because of his revolutionary ideas, he was much criticized by the contemporary Assamese society. As in Bengal, people like Jaduram and Hem Chandra had to pay the price for their liberal views. Anticipating that after his demise there would not be sufficient people to carry his dead body to the crematorium, Hem Chandra wrote that his body need not be burnt after his death, rather should be kept in a secluded area so that his body could be devoured by the vultures and crows. He was prophetic. When Hem Chandra Barua died in 1896, there were not sufficient people to carry his dead body to the crematorium.[103]

As stated earlier, a socially conscious literary circle developed in Nagaon centering the Brahmos, particularly, Gunabhiram Baruah. One such person was litterateur Ratneshwar Mahanta (1864-1893). Gunabhiram had great affection for Ratneshwar and it was essentially for him that Ratneshwar was elevated to the post of accountant. He was also a great admirer of Ratneshwar's literary talents. Ratneshwar was also close to Hem Chandra Goswami. A letter from Mahanta to Hem Chandra Goswami about the prevailing social situation in Nagaon reflects his concern. He requested Goswami to take up his pen against the dancing girls as that poses a threat for spreading venereal diseases. The letter read: "Puja has passed away. Deorgonya dancing girls have set Nagaon on fire this year. From the sucking babe to the hoary headed, everyone has been infatuated with them some has turned rather mad after them. I am ashamed to bring to your notice that some educated gentlemen of high families showed such signs of degradation in morality and deterioration of our society that the occasion in which they were present with these girls have been a topic of conversation everywhere in the town. The girls are turning as if in a steam engine—they have not a single minute's leisure in their lodging. Here one is taken away . . . there another is seen in the bosom. I am afraid that they will spread venereal diseases. . . ." The letter reflects the concern and mindset of a person who was close to Gunabhiram.[104]

Padmabati Devi Phukanani (1853-1927), who earned the unique distinction of writing the very first novel in Assamese, *Sudharmar Upakhyan*, also authored a book called *Hita-Sadhika* in 1885 which aimed at spiritual and moral uplift of the young generation. She was inspired to write this book, later recommended as a textbook in the schools of Assam, by Gunabhiram Baruah and Padmahash Goswami.[105]

Avinash Chandra Lahiri, a missionary from the Sadharan Brahmo Samaj, Calcutta, spent considerable time and energy in working among the different tribal communities of north-east India during the 1920s. He travelled extensively while preaching the Brahmo faith among the Rabhas, Garos, Mikirs and the Manipuri immigrants at Sylhet and Cachar. Though he faced difficulty in convincing the immigrant Manipuris and Mikirs about his faith, he found response among the Garos and Rabhas, and to some extent among the Kacharis of Goalpara district. In 1926 a Rabha gentleman, Dwarika Nath, wrote to the president of the Sadharan Brahma Samaj at Calcutta requesting him to extend missionary operations among them. In response, Avinash Chandra went there and succeeded in converting about 39 Garo, Rabha and Kachari women to the Brahmo faith. The Garos of Matia established a Brahmo Samaj in their village and organized Maghotsava festival for some years. They also established a primary school and made efforts to open an ME school. Those tribal people who embraced Brahmoism bound themselves to practice total abstinence or temperance.[106]

In the Brahmaputra valley, places like Nagaon, Dhubri, Dibrugarh, Tezpur and Guwahati became important centers of Brahmo activities. When Brahmo Samaj faced a split in 1878 and Keshab Chandra Sen brought forward his *NabaBidhan*, it failed to attract Assam's Brahmos. That split was reflected only at Tezpur when its secretary and the minister of Tezpur Brahmo Samaj opted to join Keshab Chandra's Bharatbarshiya Brahmo Samaj and renamed their Samaj the Brahmo Samaj of Tezpur. This decision was however opposed tooth and nail by the general members of the Samaj who started the Central Assam Upasana Samaj at Tezpur through which a concerted effort was made to spread the message of Brahmo Samaj.[107] Eight leading Brahmos of Assam published a manifesto from Tezpur against the Keshab Chandra Sen's move to split. It read: "We think that the new dispensation is a disguised form of avatarism promulgated in India from time to time and that the observances introduced in the Brahmo Samaj of India tend to encourage some form of superstition, which it should be the object of the Brahmo Samaj to root out."[108]

The Brahmo Samaj in Guwahati existed in the late 1860s. However, construction of the present temple took place much later in 1901.[109] The first Board of Trustees of the Gauhati Brahmo Samaj, which was formed in 1916 had Sarat Chandra Das, Heramba Chandra Maitra, Dr Prankrishna Acharya, Gurudas Chakravarty, Raisaheb Raj Mohan Das, Sibnath Dutta, Prasanna Chandra Dasgupta and Abhoy Charan Das as its members.[110] Prominent families of the Brahmo community of Guwahati included that of Lalit Mohan Lahiri, Hemanta Kumar Lahiri, Prabodh Kumar Lahiri, Jnanabhiram Baruah, Braja Gopal Halder, Bonolata Halder, Kiranmoy Lahiri, Dilip Kumar Lahiri, Prabhat Kumar Das, Subimal Das, Sisir Kumar Deb, Amalendu Sen, Ajay Sen, Satish Chandra Roy, Sarat Chandra Das, Heramba Chandra Maitra, Prankrishna Acharya, Gurudas Chakravarty, Raj Mohan Das, Sibnath Dutta, Kamal Lochan Das, Prasanna Chandra Das, Kailash Chandra Sen, Amiya Kumar Das and Puspalata Das, Indira Miri and Abhoy Charan Sen.

The Brahmo Samaj Mandir at Dhubri was established in 1875 and reconstructed in 1893.[111] Only these two Brahmo Samaj temples are now in existence in the entire Brahmaputra valley, carrying with it great legacies of the past.

In the Surma valley of Assam the Brahmo movement attracted a good number of people. Sylhet had a good number of Brahmo followers, and the Brahmo Samaj temple was established in 1862. Silchar also had a Brahmo Samaj although records are silent about the date of its establishment. However, according to a record a meeting of the Brahmo Samaj was held at Silchar on January 28, 1879 and Maghotsava was also celebrated that year. On April 1, 1883, the officials of the Samaj got a plot of land from the government on renewable lease for twenty years for construction of a Brahmo temple, and a temple along with a pond was completed at that site during 1897-98.[112] This is confirmed from the writings of Sivanath Sastri.[113] Initially a Board of Trustees was created with seven members to run the Brahmo Samaj at Silchar. In an extraordinary general meeting held on June 27, 1900 it was replaced by a nine member Board of Trustees.[114] It may be mentioned here that Jagat Chandra Das, senior EAC of Cachar took much initiative in the establishment of the Brahmo *mandir* at Silchar. Chitta Ranjan Das and Sivanath Sastri visited this temple soon after it was established.[115] For about half a century since 1890, Brahmo influence could be distinctly felt among a section of the educated elite and government officials of the Surma valley.

NEWS FROM ASSAM IN BRAHMO NEWS PAPERS OF CALCUTTA

Brahmo Samaj publications from Calcutta, particularly the *Brahmo Public Opinion, Sanjibani, The Indian Messenger* and *Tatwabodhini Patrika* regularly published news about various developments in Assam. Many of these news items were on socially relevant issues, especially the pathetic plight of tea garden *coolies* of Assam. The problems of clerks (*keranis*) of

Assam were for example highlighted in a letter from "Sibsagore" which read, "... Steps should have been taken for the well being of the wretched *keranis*. These under-paid persons are often required to labour more than six hours, sometimes ten to twelve, even at the government offices. Though there is a fixed time in all government offices, it is rarely observed in the *muffosils*. Even in holidays & c. the writers are called to work under the penalty of forfeiting their appointments. These things are frequently observed in the deputy commissioner's office than anywhere else.... How difficult it is to serve with a salary barely sufficient to support a man with his family ... little time is allowed for relaxation.... Some of the *Hazurs* are so very generous to refuse to grant leave for a few weeks.... We humbly beseech, that our kind government will take these into consideration and rescue the poor *keranis* from such inhumanity".[116]

News of cholera and leg disease in Sibsagar also found place in Brahmo papers at Calcutta. "Formerly cholera was unknown here (Sibsagar). Now it appears yearly and of late, monthly. Another new disease has taken root. It is called leg swelling. The very name indicates what sort of a disease it is. The civil medical officer ascribes it to the bazar oil," reported a Brahmo newspaper.[117] The same issue of the paper also reported on a cyclone at Nazira, conclusion of the monsoon sky race at Sibsagar and change of name of the Zilla School to the Sibsagar High English School.[118]

"With the approval of the Government of India, the Chief Commissioner is pleased to notify that that headquarters of the district of Goalpara have been transferred from the station of Goalpara to the station at Dhubri, with effect from the 24th instant, on which date the district treasury was opened at Dhubri," reports the same newspaper.[119]

A memorandum expressing the grievances of the zamindars of Goalpara against the Assam Local Rates Regulation was not only reported in the Brahmo Press, but some papers also came out with editorial comments on the issue. Supporting the Goalpara zamindars *The Indian Messenger* wrote "the memorial that the Goalpara zamindars addressed to the Government of India need serious consideration by the authorities concerned as the rate fixed has been arbitrary and unjust."[120] ". . . They (the Goalpara zamindars) very justly complain that whereas in Bengal the Public Works cess is levied for the purpose of famine relief only, in Assam they would be applicable also to local purpose. . . . Whereas in Bengal the Public Works cess is levied upon the gross collection, in Assam an arbitrary rate of Rs.2 per acre has been fixed, and they show that the gross collection does not exceed 8 annas per acre. We hope the Government of India will give careful consideration to the memorial, and meet the just demands of the Assam zamindars," commented *The Brahmo Public Opinion.*[121]

Letters suggesting how to tackle alcoholism in the tea gardens of Assam also appeared in these newspapers. One such interesting letter read, "I find from your last issue that the Cachar tea planters are crying out loud against the ravages of the outstill system among the coolies, and that the Chief Commissioner's remedy is to get the planters themselves to become Outstillers! I would suggest an improvement, or an amendment. Do away with the cheap and nasty outstill liquor altogether and get good sadar distilled spirits to be sold to the coolies at a proper price. . . . The only real remedy for drunkenness among the poor in India is to raise the price of liquor as high as possible so as to be beyond the reach of temptation of the mass of people, but as long as the out-stills are in vogue, that is impossible. . . ."[122]

The grievance against the European District Engineer of Jorhat was also reported in the Brahmo Press: "The inhabitants of the Jorehat subdivision are greatly aggrieved by and dissatisfied with the result of the working of the local Board. The native members find it impossible to do their duties towards their constituencies owing to the negligence and unwillingness of the District Engineer to carry out their projects. The District Engineer has practically reduced the Board to a mere subordinate body. It is hoped that the leading members Messrs Bezbaruah and Borah will bring the whole state of affairs to the notice of the Government. Unless Government strengthens the authority of the local Boards, they will prove a mere show, specially when they will have to deal with European officers."[123]

The Indian Association where most of the important office bearers were Brahmo activists in the early part of 1880s, not only took up the coolie problem in right earnest (discussed later), it also took up for discussion the cause of higher education in Assam. In its annual report of 1880, the Indian Association expressed its very serious concern that "in Assam the only high school of the province has been suppressed."[124] Wholeheartedly supporting the memorial submitted by the *Assam Hitakari Sabha* on the subject to the Governor of Assam, *Brahmo Public Opinion* reported, "The *Assam Hitakari Sabha* has submitted a memorial to the Chief Commissioner of Assam for the reestablishment of college classes of the Gauhati High School which were abolished in 1876. We regret we cannot make room for the memorial that seems to us very well-drawn; and the facts and arguments used by our brethren in this memorial seems to us to be almost unanswerable. It is indeed a pity that there should not be a college in the whole Assam, and that the students who are poor, should have to come to Bengal to complete their education. The effect has been this: out of 24 Assamese students who passed the entrance examination since 1875 about one-third could not prosecute their studies, although six of them had obtained scholarships. The memorial shows that while nine Assamese students passed the first Arts from the Gauhati High School during the eight years of existence, not more that two passed the same examination from the other schools since the abolition of college classes.... We cannot but sufficiently commend the laudable efforts of the memorialists in the cause of high education, and we hope Sir Stuart Baylay will grant their prayer."[125] Reports to liberate some ladies from the clutches of the *aarkathis* (middlemen and recruiting agents) and planters also regularly appeared in the Brahmo newspapers.[126]

It is true that unlike in Bengal, the Brahmo Samaj ideals did not percolate down to the grassroots, but it no doubt had important bearing on the socio-religious history of the region. It is through the Brahmo Samaj movement that the effects of the so-called Bengal renaissance could be felt in the Brahmaputra valley.[127] In analysing the germination of the new political order in Assam during 1853-73, eminent historian Amalendu Guha observes that "it was precisely because of this reason that, despite a conflict of interests between the immigrant Bengali *baboos* and the indigenous *dangoriyas* for administrative jobs, their mutual relations had not yet been embittered to the extent it was to be in later times. Assamese and immigrant Bengali adherents to the Brahmo Samaj had a social impact in the growing administrative townships."[128] Rajen Saikia opines that by introducing some significant aesthetic values in social, cultural and religious life, the Brahmo Samaj exercised a wholesome effect on Assamese life. It helped to reduce the hold of orthodoxy in society and for the first time made religious faith an object of doubt and debate. It also popularized the professional life of the new middle class."[129]

Two other very important aspects of the Brahmo Samaj's contribution to the north-east—in the Khasi and Jaintia hills and among the tea garden labourers in Assam—have unfortunately not been highlighted either in official or private publications of recent years. It thus becomes imperative to explore these two forgotten chapters of history of the north-east.

Notes and References

1. Amalendu Guha Impact of Bengal Renaissance on Assam 1825-75, *Indian Economic and Social History Review*, Vol. IX, September 9, 1992, p. 292. Adam White referred by Guha.
2. Devendra Nath Tagore, *Atmajibani* [first published in 1898 from Calcutta], Reprint, Calcutta, 1968, pp. 147-48.
3. Sivanath Sastri, *History of Brahmo Samaj* [first published in 1911 from Calcutta], Reprint, Calcutta, 1993, pp. 518-19.
4. Gunabhiram was awarded the title of *Raibahadur* in 1887 during the 50th coronation ceremony of Queen Victoria.

5. Gunabhiram Barua, *Anandaram Dhekial Phukanar Jiban Charita* [first printed in 1880], Guwahati, 1917, pp. 176-77.
6. Sivanath Sastri, *Atmacharita* [first published in 1918 from Calcutta], Third Edition, 1940, pp. 156-57.
7. *Orunodoi* was the first literary magazine-cum-newspaper which was published from Sivasagar in upper Assam by the Christian Baptist Missionaries since 1846.
8. Maheswar Neog ed., *Orunodoi* (1846-1886), Guwahati, 1983. (See May 1853 and December 1853 issues.)
9. Ji Ra, *"Puruse Tirotak Ji Rupe Samadar Karibo Lage"*, *Orunodoi*, October 1856, p. 155; Gunabhiram wrote a number of articles under different pen names like *Ji Ra, Ejan Asamiya lok etc.*
10. Gunabhiram Barua under the pen name *'Ejan Asamiya Lok'*, *"Bibahar Samayat Ji Sakal Niyam Pratipalan Kara Kartabya Tar Katha"*, *Orunodoi*, December 1853, pp. 185-88.
11. *Dujani Bidhaba Chowalir Bibaha Howar Katha, Orunodoi,* January 1857, pp. 6-7.
12. Gunabhiram Baruah's series of articles on the related subject were published in *Orunodoi* between May 1853 and April 1858.
13. Jatindra Mohan Bhattacharya ed.. *Ramnavami Natak,* 1372, *Bangabda*, Calcutta, p. 6.
14. Sivnath Barman, *Asamiya Jibani Abhidhan,* Guwahati, 1992, p. 75.
15. Raj Narayan Basu, *Atmacharit,* Sixth Edition, Calcutta, p. 55. It is interesting to note that Padmahash's uncle addressed Rajnarayan as the "*Vyasdeva of Kali Yuga*".
16. *Brahmo Public Opinion,* Calcutta, May 22, 1879.
17. *Ibid.*, Calcutta, April 24, 1879.
18. Sivanath Sastri, *History of the Brahmo Samaj,* originally published in 1911, Reprint, Calcutta, 1993, pp. 518-19.
19. *Brahmo Public Opinion,* July 18, 1878, Calcutta.
20. *The Indian Messenger,* March 31, 1894. See obituary reference on Gunabhiram Baruah's demise. Also, Tilottama Misra, *Swarnalata,* Guwahati, 1997, pp. 48-49.
21. Sivanath Sastri, *Atmacharit*, 3rd edition, Calcutta, 1940, p. 347.
22. *Brahmo Public Opinion,* 15th August 1878.
23. *Ibid.*
24. *Ibid.*, 12th September 1878.
25. *Ibid.*, 8th April 1880.
26. *Ibid.*, 6th May 1880.
27. The subjects of his speeches delivered during his visit in 1887 could not be traced though there are evidences that he delivered speeches at Dhubri, Guwahati and Shillong in 1887.
28. Lakshminath Bezbarua, *Mor Jibon Sonwaran*, Dibrugarh, 1998 edn., pp. 64-65.

29. Bezbarua, *Ibid.*
30. Kanailal Chottopadhaya, *Asame Cha Coolie Andolon O Ramkumar Vidyaratna*, Calcutta, 1989, p. 168.
31. Prasenjit Choudhury, *Asamer Cha Banua aru Unobingsha Satikar Vidyat Samaj*, Dibrugarh, 1989, pp. 97-164.
32. Both *Udasin Satyasrabar Assam Bharaman* and *Assam Bhraman* are rare books and are preserved at India Office Library, London.
33. *Brahmo Public Opinion*, April 11, 1878, Calcutta.
34. H.K. Barpujari, *Asamar Naba Jagaran, Ana-Asamiyar Bhumika*, Jorhat.
35. W.W. Hunter, *Statistical Account of Assam*, 1879, Reprint 1998, p. 35.
36. Census of India, Report 1901, p. 46.
37. Sarada Manjari Dutta, *Mahajatrar Pathey, Bangabda* 1348, Calcutta, p. 130.
38. Prafulla Ch. Barua, *Asamat Batori Kakat: Eti Ruprekha*, Guwahati, 1993, p. 298.
39. Sivnath Barman, *Asamiya Jivani Abhidhan*, Guwahati, 1992, p. 266.
40. *Assam Bandhu*, 1885, pp. 2-3.
41. Nanda Talukdar, *Sambad Patrar Kanchiali Rodat Asomiya Sahitya*, Guwahati, 1975, p. 15.
42. Jogendra Narayan Bhuyan, ed., *Ratneswar Mahanta Rachanabali*, Guwahati, 1977, p. 3.
43. Tilottama Misra, *Swarnalata*, Guwahati, 1997, p. 199.
44. *Digvijaya* and *Gyanodoi* have not been incorporated in the works of Sivaprasad Barua, Satyendra Nath Sarma and Prafulla Ch. Barua, who have made pioneering contribution towards the history of journalism in Assam.
45. Report on the Administration of the Province of Assam for the year 1874-75 and 1875-76. See relevant portions related to press.
46. Jogendra Narayan Bhuyan, *Uoli Joa Nathir Pora*, Nagaon, 1991, p. 85.
47. Bhuyan, *op. cit.*, p. 84, Bhuyan informs that each of the books was priced at Rupee one.
48. Sivanath Barman, *op. cit.*, p. 153.
49. Chandraprasad Saikia ed., *Radhanath Changkakoti*, Guwahati, 1971, see articles by Bhimkanto Konwar, p. 87.
50. *Ibid.*, see articles by Indubhusan Chakraborty.
51. Prafulla Chandra Barua, *op. cit.*, p. 298.
52. H.K. Barpujari observed that Kamalakanta was termed as a "*Mlechha*" by the contemporary society [H.K. Barpujari ed., *The Comprehensive History of Assam*, Vol. V, Guwahati, 1993, p. 200].
53. Rajen Saikia, *Social and Economic History of Assam*, New Delhi, 2001, p. 209.
54. Letter in *The Indian Messenger*, dated 6 November, 1890.
55. Tilottama Misra, *Literature and Society in Assam*, Guwahati, 1987, pp. 113-14.

56. *Brahmo Public Opinion* circulation statement, 21st October 1894.
57. Shiela Borthakur, *Lekhikar Jibani*, Guwahati, 1987, p. 26. Also Sivnath Barman, *op. cit.*, pp. 74-75, 191.
58. Hem Borah, *Asamiya Sahitya Loi Mahila Lekhakar Dan*, Golaghat, 1994, p. 34.
59. Chandra Prasad Saikia ed., *Lakshminath Bezbaruah,* Guwahati, 1968, Reprint 1981, p. 13 and Sivnath Barman, *op. cit.*, p. 163; also Dipankar Banerjee's article on *Pragnasundari Devi* in *The Telegraph*, Guwahati *Bihu Special Supplement,* 2004.
60. Atul Ch. Hazarika ed., *Bezbaruah Granthabali,* Vol. II, Guwahati 1968, pp. 1381-84.
61. *Brahmo Public Opinion,* April 24, 1879.
62. Tilottama Misra, *Swarnalata*, p. 189. Also Sivanath Shastri, *History of Brahmo Samaj,* Calcutta, 1911, p. 579.
63. Late Santimoy Dasgupta used to teach at Sishu Pathsala Higher Secondary School at Dhubri. A devoted Brahmo, Santimoy lived with his elder sister, a popular doctor. Santimoy had a good collection of all letters and diaries that he inherited from his forefathers. They included a letter from Rabindranath Tagore and a letter from Sivanath Sastri that were shown to the author in course of discussion in 1979.
64. Several such reports appeared in *Brahmo Public Opinion*, Calcutta during 1870s.
65. *The Indian Messenger,* Calcutta, July 27, 1884.
66. Dipankar Banerjee, "Remembering Tagores Assam Connection", *The Telegraph,* Calcutta, May 11, 1998. Also see Tilottama Misra, *Swarnalata, op. cit.*
67. Rajen Saikia, *Social and Economic History of India*, New Delhi, 2000, pp. 209-10.
68. Sudhir Mukherjee, *Mahapran Ramesh Chandra Mukherjee*, Calcutta, 1956, pp. 5-6. The booklets mentions how Ambikacharan died in the premises of the Dhubri Brahmo Samaj premices on July 2, 1902 while conducting a prayer. Almost the entire male population of the small town attended Ambikacharan's funeral as his death during the prayer was interpreted as his was a great soul.
69. See summary of education reports, Public Instruction Department, Eastern Bengal and Assam 1901. A copy of the report, now brittle, is available at the Dhubri District Library.
70. Tilottama Misra, *op. cit.*, p. 80.
71. The school has been renamed now as Raja Rammohan Roy Nursery School that is being nurtured and supervised by Smt. Ila Chakraborty at present.
72. Mention may be made of articles like *Karmeti Bai* [*Assam Bandhu*, Fagun 1885, Vol. I, pp. 81-85], *Prakrita Laj Ki* [*Assam Bandhu*, Chot, 1886, Vol. 14, pp. 105-8] and *Jatodharmostatojaya* [Jonaki 3rd year, 2nd issue] written by Swarnalata Devi.

73. Ananda Chandra Agarwalla's article "*Asamiya Sahitya Sevakini*", *Awahan,* 4th year, 5th issue, 1931, p. 515.
74. Hemo Bora, *Asomiya Sahitya Loi Mahila Lekhakar Dan,* Golaghat, 1994, p. 37.
75. Sivanath Barman, *op. cit.*, p. 272; also Kashinath Barman, *Nari Ratna,* Guwahati, 1986.
76. Nagen Saikia ed., *Assam Bandhu,* p. 23.
77. *Assam Bandhu,* Vol. II, pp. 381-86.
78. Sivanath Barman ed., *Asamiya Jatiyo Abhidhan*.
79. Sheela Borthakur, *Lekhikar Joboni,* Guwahati, 1987.
80. Sibnath Barman ed., *Asamiya Jatiyo Abhidhan*.
81. Gairika Barua Ahmed, *Heroa Bahir Sur*, Guwahati, 2005.
82. *Ibid.*
83. *Ibid.*
84. Author's interview with Nirupama Bargohain, noted literateur of Assam. Punyaprabha Barua taught Nirupama Bargohain in the school. A manogenerian Punyaprabha stays at Jorpukhuri of Guwahati (in 2006).
85. *Ibid.* and *Heroa Bahir Sur, op. cit.*
86. *Ibid.*
87. For detailed account of this defamation case see Jatin Das's articles in *Ajir Asom*; published from Guwahati, also author's discussion with Nirupama Buragohain at Guwahati on the subject; also *Heroa Bahir Sur, op. cit*.
88. *Heroa Bahir Sur*; also see *Gariyashi*, Nirupama Bargohain's review on *Heroa Bahir Sur*, Guwahati, May, 2006, pp. 16-19.
89. Amalendu Guha, *Planter Raj to Swaraj,* New Delhi, 1979, p. 65, also Sivnath Barman, *op. cit.*, p. 266.
90. Udayan Misra, *The Transformation of Assamese Identity: A Historical Survey,* Shillong, 2001, p. 25.
91. *Banhi,* Vol. I, No. 2, Saka, 1831.
92. Udayan Misra, *op. cit.*, p. 24.
93. Sudhir Chandra, *The Oppressive Present: Literature and Consciousness in Colonial India,* New Delhi, 1994, p. 67.
94. Letter No. 1349, dt. April 14, 1890 cited in the Proceedings of the Chief Commissioner of Assam in the Notification, General Dept. No. 3835/1/ 2G, dated June 4, 1890.
95. Sudhir Mukherjee, *op. cit.*, p. 16.
96. *Ibid.*, p. 14.
97. Nilmani Chakravarty, *Atmajivansmriti,* Calcutta, Bangabda 1327, Reprint, Bangabda 1382, pp. 85-86.
98. K.S. Singh, *Tribal Movements in India,* New Delhi, 1982, Vol. I, p. 24.
99. For further details on the subject See R.N. Mosahary, "Brahmo Religion and Social Change among the Boros", *Proceedings of the North-East India History Association*, Shillong, 1885, pp. 347-52.
100. Atul Chandra Hazarika, *Smritir Papori*, Guwahati, 1977, pp. 12-13.

101. J. Goswami ed., *Asamiya Sahityer Chaneki*, Vol. III, Part I, p. 177.
102. Padmanath Gohain Baruah, *Jibani Sangraha*, Part II, p. 48.
103. Nanda Talukder, *Jiwan Smaran*, Guwahati, 1981; also Padmanath Gohain Baruah ed., *Jiwani Sangraha*, Guwahati, p. 163.
104. Letter of Ratneshwar Mahanta to Hem Chandra Goswami, dt. 24th October 1888 cited in Jogendra Nath Bhuyan ed., *Ratneshwar Mahanta Rachanavali*, Guwahati, 1977, p. 344. Ratneshwar wrote some interesting articles in *Assam Bandhu* which include "Garo Brittanta", "Swadhinata ne Swechhachar" etc.
105. *Awahan*, Ananda Chandra Agarwalla's articles, *op. cit.*; also Shila Barthakur, *Lekhir Jibani*, p. 27; *Sudharmar Upakhyan* was pub...hed in 1884 from 20/1 Cornwallis Street, Calcutta and was printed by Bhuban Chandra Ghosh. Priced at 4 annas per copy the novel contained 42 pages in six chapters. Her other book *Hitasadhika*, published in 1885, was priced at 1 anna per copy.
106. Lakshmi Narayan Roy ed., Brahmo Samaj, *Depressed Classes and Untouchability*, first published in 1933, Second edn. Calcutta, 1996, pp. 66-67.
107. *Brahmo Public Opinion*, Calcutta, December 12, 1878; also Sashtri, *op. cit.*, p. 519.
108. Sashtri, *op. cit.*, pp. 519-20.
109. This old temple has been demolished and a beautiful new temple complex was built in 1998.
110. The Board of Trustees of Gauhati Brahmo Samaj was changed in 1940, 1958, 1995 and 2000. Between 1940 and 2006, following members served the Board of Trustees: Lalit Mohan Das, Satish Chandra Das, Prabodh Kumar Lahiri, Rajen Chandra Sarkar, Girija Kumar Das, Amar Chandra Bhattacharjee, Birendra Chandra Chakravarty, Prabhat Kumar Das, Kiranmoy Lahiri, Subimal Das, Braja Gopal Halder, Sisir Kumar Dey, Dr. Amalendu Sen, Ajay Kumar Sen, Anjali Lahiri, Puspalata Das, Minati Chanda, Dr. Basana Rajan Halder. The present Board of Trustees (formed in 2000) of Gauhati Brahmo Samaj include Dr. Basana Ranjan Halder (President), Krishnanjan Chanda (Secretary), Anjali Lahiri, Puspalata Das, Minati Chanda, Dr. Ardhendu Banerjee, Rukma Sen, Dr. Dipankar Banerjee, Dr. Anima Guha, Dr. Mukti Dev Chowdhury and Sheila Dutta, Bipash Ranjan Halder, Samarendra Nath Das and Ashoke Chowdhury.
111. *Brahmo Prarthana Samajes in India*, a booklet published by Andhra Brahmo Samaj and Hyderabad Deccan Brahma Samaj, Hyderabad, 1996, pp. 21-25.
112. This Brahmo Samaj temple was however dismantled in 1968 and women's college established in the premises.
113. Sivanath Sastri, *Sadhanaasramer Itibritta*, 1952, Reprint, Calcutta, 1992, p. 57.

114. The members of the Board were Abhaya Charan Das, Raj Chandra Chowdhury, Sadaya Charan Das, Kamini Kumar Chanda, Raj Chandra Das, Jagat Chandra Dev, Madan Mohan Dutta, Govinda Narayan Singha and Sarada Charan Nandy.
115. Debabrata Dutta's article on *Cachar Brahmo Samaj* published in *Purbasree*, Silchar, pp. 35-38.
116. *Brahmo Public Opinion*, Calcutta, March 27, 1879.
117. *Ibid.*, Calcutta, June 26, 1879.
118. *Ibid.*
119. *Ibid.*
120. *The Indian Messenger*, Calcutta, May 21, 1880.
121. *Brahmo Public Opinion*, Calcutta, June 3, 1880.
122. *The Indian Messenger*, Calcutta, May 3, 1885.
123. *Ibid.*, June 21, 1885.
124. The full text of the Annual Report of the Indian Association appeared in *Brahmo Public Opinion*, on March 25, 1880.
125. *Brahmo Public Opinion*, Calcutta, 1 July, 1880.
126. See Appendix for a similar report.
127. Amalendu Guha, "Impact of Bengal Renaissance on Assam 1825-75", *Indian Economic and Social History Review*, September, 1972 Issue.
128. Amalendu Guha, *Planter Raj to Swaraj Freedom Struggle and Electoral Politics in Assam 1826-1947*, New Delhi, 1977, Reprint 1988, p. 23.
129. Rajen Saikia, *Social and Economic History of Assam*, New Delhi, 2000, p. 210.

2

BRAHMO ACTIVITIES IN THE KHASI HILLS

Brahmo movement entered the Khasi hills both through the northern and the southern routes immediately after the shifting of the Secretariat at Shillong in 1874. Some government officials who were transferred from Sylhet i.e., from the South of Khasi hills came and settled at Shillong. Similarly, a number of Brahmo believers also came from the north of Khasi hills, through Guwahati, to settle at Shillong. Gradually a section of the settlers as well as a small section of the Khasi people became responsive to the ideas of Brahmo Samaj. Among the agencies which played important catalytic role in the emancipation of the Khasi society towards the end of the nineteenth century, Brahmo Samaj was one.

The first Brahmo Samaj of Shillong was established in 1874—the very year when the town became the political headquarter of the province. Unlike the Brahmaputra valley where a number of Brahmo missionaries like Aghorenath, Ramkumar Vidyaratna or Dwarakanath Ganguly visited and spread the messages of Brahmo faith during 1870s and 1880s, in the Khasi Hills the movement spread because of the initiative taken by some officials who came to Shillong on government assignments. In fact after the establishment of Shillong as the political headquarter of the British Raj, this far eastern village of India, which soon developed into a town, had experienced significant changes in social, religious and other spheres. Raj Chandra Chowdhury and Brajendra Nath Sen, two government officials who came to Shillong were mainly instrumental in starting the Brahmo Samaj activities at Shillong. Lalmadhar Basu, Tarini Charan Nandy and pandit Kailash Nath Sen joined them soon.

Though a Samaj was established, construction of a temple took some time. The prayers were conducted at the houses of different Brahmos by rotation till the first Brahmo Samaj prayer hall (Mandir) was established in November, 1874. The activities of the Brahmo Samaj members, their life style, their care and concern for the local people could gradually attract some people from the local Khasi community.

Among the early Khasi gentlemen who were attracted towards the Brahmo faith, mention may be made of Job Solomon and Radhan Singh. They were quite convinced about the progressive ideas of the Brahmos and took initiative to purchase a ready made house at Mawkhar where they set up a Brahmo Samaj *Mandir* in 1886. This Mawkhar Brahmo Samaj *Mandir* was the first community prayer hall established at the initiative of local Khasi Brahmo converts of the Hills, which is in the province of Meghalaya now. "In connection with their office works Job Solomon and Radhan Singh came to know about the Brahmo religion. Five Bengalis and two Khasi gentlemen purchased a house at Mowkhar, a Khasi locality, and established a Brahmo Samaj there. For that purpose they had to take loan. Here they met every Saturday for Brahmo prayers. The service was mainly conducted in Khasi language. Babu Tarini Charan Nandy and Radhan Singh jointly translated some Brahmo prayers into Khasi language", writes Nilmani Chakravarty, a Brahmo missionary in Khasi hills who rendered yeomen service activities towards the Khasi people.[1] Some Bengali gentlemen also tried to establish a bigger prayer hall and mobilized fund for this purpose around the same time. *The Indian Messenger* reported in 1883: "The Shillong Brahmo Samaj are in urgent need of a Prayer House which will require about Rs. 5,000/-. Prakash Chandra Dev and Raj Chandra Chowdhury of Shillong Brahmo Samaj now in Calcutta have been authorized to retain donation which may be forwarded to them direct".[2]

By the end of the nineteenth century, a good number of Brahmo Samaj followers began to reside at Shillong—most of them came there on government jobs. This group included Sivnath Dutta, Prakash Chandra Dev, Bharat Chandra Chowdhury, Mathuranath Nandy, Ramgati Das, Harikishore Sarma, Ishwar Chandra Pal, Satish Ch. Sen, Baikuntha Nath Dutta, Sanat Kumar Das, Sadaya Charan Das, Anathbandhu Sen and others. For the sake of commonality of spiritual faith, most of the people of the Brahmo faith decided to settle at Laban area of Shillong and that is how a *Brahmo Pally* was established at Laban in the last decade of the nineteenth century. Some of the later prominent Brahmo activists at Shillong, apart from the names mentioned above, included Bharat Chandra Chowdhury, Gurucharan Sen and Umesh Chandra Chowdhury.

Gradually the *Brahmo Pally* of Laban at Shillong became a hub of Brahmo activities and Brahmo festivals were organized there with much funfare. "The 9th anniversary of Shillong Brahmo Samaj took place with much funfare on 8 November last and the festival extended upto 11th of the month. . . . The programme was singularly enthusiastic. . . . The procession through the streets on the concluding day was specially successful. As they issued forth our last anniversary hymn, a divine enthusiasm filled the band, and every heart melted away in the name of God. After their return to the place of worship, where every available creek and corner was filled with people, a lecture was delivered by Babu Raj Chandra Chowdhury, whose appeal was so earnest and effective, that no sooner had it concluded, than two young men of the place came forward to make a public confession of their faith in Brahmoism, and to become publicly initiated to the faith. May God sustain the spiritual life of this little community !" reported *The Indian Messenger*.[3]

Several schools were established by the Brahmos at Shillong and other places of Khasi Hills in the last quarter of the nineteenth century. Sivnath Dutta established a school at Laban. Another school was started at Laban namghar where pandit Kailash Chandra Sen used to teach. To impart value-based quality education to the children of Shillong, with focus on moral spiritual and scientific education, another school was established in the same locality where Hemanta Kumari Devi served as the founder Secretary and Sarada Manjari Devi served as a teacher.

Soon a school was also established at Mawkhar Brahmo Samaj at the initiative of Jeebon Roy and enlightened Khasi gentleman. That the Brahmo community was a growing body in Khasi and Jaintia Hills could be evidenced from the fact that by 1900 there were seven branches of Brahmo Samaj in different parts of the Hills.In 1889 some Bengali Brahmos of Shillong published a leaflet in the Khasi language on the cardinal principle of the Brahmo Samaj. Jeeban Roy was closely associated with the other Bengali Brahmo families of Shillong and established a very good rapport with them.[4] Early Khasi Brahmo social activists included U Thiam Singh, U Rushan Singh, U. Simiyan, U Holi Singh, U Bishnu, U Hindromoni, U Singh Manik, U. Krishna, U Barkrishna, Rohini Kanta Roy, U Ba Singh and U Tham Singh. Maharshi Devendra Nath Tagore was much impressed at their work.[5] We find from records that as the number of people for prayers at the Mowkhar Brahmo Samaj (which was attended mainly by the people from the Khasi community) was increasing gradually and it was reported that, "seven-eight new benches were ordered to accommodate the increasing number".[6]

The first library exclusively for the use of women in undivided Assam named Rammohan Mahila Pustakalaya (Library) was established by a Brahmo activist Smt. Hemanta Kumari Devi at Shillong in 1887. Hemanta Kumari was the wife of Raj Chandra Chowdhury. To her also goes the unique distinction of establishing the first Indian women's organization of north-east India—The *Mahila Samity*, at Jail Road, Shillong in1874.[7] This *Mahila Samity*, which by 1887 started working in full swing and appointed its office bearers, was destined to play a very important role towards the upliftment of socio-cultural life of Shillong for nearly a century.

Initially its members used to meet once a week. Its aim was to make "collective effort for the spiritual and moral upliftment of the local ladies, sharing knowledge and encourage fellow feeling among the ladies of all communities at Shillong" The door of the Samiti was open to the ladies of all communities. The Samiti also opened a kindergarten school for the children of three to six years age group.[8] Infact the Rammohan Mahila Library was later run by this *Mahila Samiti*. The Library was ultimately shifted to the Khasi Hills Brahma Samaj complex, in its own building at Laban on 28 January, 1922 and remains functional till now.[9]

Being inspired by the Brahmo Samaj activities at Shillong and after coming to know about the Brahmo faith from a small leaflet in Khasi language which incorporated the cardinal principle of Brahmo Samaj,[10] three Khasi gentlemen—Krishnadhan, Join Manik and Joggeswar, all residents of Shella, approached the Brahmo activists of Shillong to send some representatives of the Samaj to take up missionary activities in the southern part of the Khasi hills and to explain the teachings of Brahmoism. The application was forwarded to the Sadharan Brahmo Samaj, Calcutta. Shivnath Sastri took personal initiative to send Nilmani Chakravarty—who was then working as his assistant at Sadharan Brahmo Samaj, Calcutta to Shillong in June 1889 to carry out missionary activities among the Khasi people, initially for a period of few months.

This thirty year old young gentleman, Nilmani was destined to play an important role in the Khasi and Jaintia hills. He arrived at Shillong on 12 June, 1889 and immediately started his missionary work with philanthropic zeal. Nilmani decided that he should live among the Khasis and started to learn the Khasi language from them. Within a short time of three months he picked up the language quite well and decided to deliver the sermons in Khasi language. On 15 September, 1889 Nilmani delivered his divine services in Khasi language. Soon he got the service book and hymns in Khasi printed from Calcutta. However much before Nilmani's arrival the local Brahmos took initiative to get the main teachings of Brahmo faith printed in Khasi language which were distributed among the local people. But the manuscript for conducting the Divine services among the Khasis was later revised by a Khasi gentleman and was reprinted at Calcutta at Nilmani Chakravarty's initiative again in 1890.

Nilmani Chakravarty now decided to go the interior village for missionary work and to leave Shillong. He felt that the message of Brahmo faith must be spread to the grassroots. Nilmani arrived at Cherrapunjee in September,1889 and took initiative to set up a Brahmo mission there. In this work he got the whole-hearted cooperation and support right from the very beginning from two local Khasi gentlemen—Job Soloman and Tham Singh of Cherra. Tham Singh was a Unitarian who helped Nilmani in his work all through. From Cherrapunjee he went to Shella and started his activities in right earnest as he was convinced that the work in the hills would bear abundant fruit. Soon two missions were established at Shella. He established a Brahmo Prayer Hall at Mousmai on a donation of Rs. Fifty sent by Durga Mohan Das for this purpose. For construction of the Cherrapunji Mission Hall an amount of Rupees three hundred and fifty was spent, informs Nilmani.[11]

Shella became the center of Nilmanibabu's work for some time. Some interesting incidents have been recorded by Nilmani in his biography. At the request of a vaisnavite convert to Brahmoism Nilamani translated two Bengali *sankirtans* to Khasi, set them to music and taught them how to sing them. As supporting instruments for *sankirtan, Khol and kartals* were introduced instead of *dhol*; but people did not like these *sankirtans* which were sung in processions. "In certain places of the Khasi hills the Khasis learnt from goldsmiths and other people of the lower orders from the sylhet district to dance and sing vulgar songs to the accompaniment of *dhol*. Partially because of this reason and partly at the instigation of the Christians, there had sprung up among the Khasis a dislike for Bengali tunes. Hence at first some difficulties were experienced in introducing and popularizing Brahmo hymns", wrote Nilmani Chakravarty.[12]

Gradually Nilmani was convinced that in addition to his

preaching work he should take steps to render medical aid to the people in the rural area. He knew homoeopathy. The Khasi people were generally not accustomed to take medicines. For curing themselves from ailments they believed in nature cure or were dependent on some of the traditional herbs. Initially, Nilmani had to make a lot of efforts to persuade the Khasis to take medicines. However within a short time the people of interior Cherrapunjee, Shella etc. understood the effictiveness of homoeopathic medicine given by Nilmani and soon patients began to come from distant places, particularly on the market days. During cholera epidemics, Nilmani used to go round the villages with his medicine box. Nilmani wrote in his autobiography that in those days often when cholera broke out in the villages, soon it used to take the form of an epidemic and very often hundreds used to flee away from their villages in panic. On occasions he gave shelter to cholera infected people in his house and nursed them. "When epidemics broke out, the hill people became so panicky that no assistance was rendered to the affected people by their co-villagers. Once a woman whose husband, daughter and grandchildren had died of cholera in course of a week, left for home in panic, and finding no shelter anywhere, took refuge in the courtyard of Nilmani Babu's quarter.... With some difficulty shelter was provided for them, and medical aid rendered. They recovered, stayed for a month and a half, and then went away. Frequently patients found lying on the public roads in a serious condition and had been given shelter and treated. For such homeless and helpless patients, and also for those who came for treatment from distant villages, a house with three rooms had to be built in the Cherrapoonji Mission Compound. Two rooms were allotted to the patients, while a poor Brahmo was allowed to occupy the third free of charge, as caretaker of the house", wrote observers.[13]

Nilmani became a true friend of the Khasis. Sivnath Sastri observed: "Within a short time the hill people began to look upon him as their true friend and benefactor and men and women began to flock to the services of the Samaj. The movement has grown ever since, till the number of Brahmos who have joined the communion has risen to nearly 500. Samajes have come to be established amongst the hill people in other stations than Cherrapunji. The number of these branch Samajes has come up to 12 up to this time [1911] and Brahmoism may be fairly said to have taken root amongst these people. Almost all these branch Samajes have a variety of institutions attached to them for propagatory and other work all carried on by the Khasis themselves, a great proof of the success of the Mission".[14]

After the earthquake of 1897, there was a fever epidemic in the entire hills and people began to die in hundreds. Immediately Nilmani along with his dedicated team of Brahmo followers swang into action and began to nurse hundreds of people who were injured. While thanking Nilmani for the excellent service he rendered to the local people, Yuvaraj Chandra Singh of Cherrapoonji wrote to him to come to a particular village in Cherrapoonji to treat the people. Nilmani suggested that the King should appeal to the Government to send a doctor first. Nilmani drafted the application for the King. This advice was at the root of the establishment of a Government Charitable dispensary at Cherrapunji. It may be mentioned here that every Brahmo Mission worker in the Khasi Hills was given lessons about diseases and their treatment.

During this period of disaster, Nilmani extensively toured Shella and adjoining villages with money, medicine and old clothes. The Unitarian Mission of England helped Nilmani in his relief work by sending a handsome amount of money. There were frequent after shocks of the earthquake. The village of Shella had slid down hill, many inhabitants were killed. Disease followed the catastrophe. Every hut there had a number of patients. The two European missionaries who also used to distribute medicines could not cope with the pressure and had left the village. There were eight to ten deaths daily but there were nobody to cremate the dead bodies. Along with a handful of dedicated Brahmos, Nilmani arranged their cremation for several weeks following the earthquake.[15]

The Syem of Cherra, Hajan Manick Syiem gave Nilmani a plot of land at Mawkisim, bordering the British territory for building a school and a prayer hall which were established in 1892.[16] Shortly sixteen Brahmo Mission centers were set up in different villages with the help of local Brahmo workers. Rohini Kanta Roy of Shella helped Nilmani to build schools and prayer halls in Barapunji, Mawsmai, Nongthymmai, Upper Cherrapunji, Mowlang and Laitkensew. The DPI visited Nilmani's school at Cherrapunji which was considered an honour those days. Devendranath Tagore received Nilmani with open arms and as a mark of his sympathy placed in his hands a respectable sum as his donation and also went on regularly helping him.[17] Subsequently some more schools were opened at Disong, Sohlap and Mooston.

Most of the books which were taught in the schools of Khasi Hills were non-secular in character as almost all these books were prepared by the Welsh missionaries. The Unitarians, the Brahmos, the Roman Catholic Missions and the native community at large were denied the right of representation in the Text Book Committee. The government policy was entire abstinence from interference with the religious instruction in aided schools. Nilmani took up the cause of secular education and at last the Chief Commissioner advised that the Welsh Mission would do well, as a body aided by government to abstain from aggressively asserting its position as Mission schools were state aided.[18]

Cherrapunjee mission established by Nilmani gradually became the most important center for Brahmo Mission activities. Rohini Kanta, Simiyan and Holi Roy were closely associated with this Khasi mission. When Nilmani met Simiyan he was quite old. Previously Simiyan was a Christian who gradually was attracted to Brahmo faith. Later, a Brahmo Prayer hall was established at his residence. In his autobiography Nilmani Chakravarty mentions that in this Brahmo prayer hall seven persons, including two ladies, formally joined Brahmo samaj. Five more Khasi ladies formally joined the Samaj around the same time at Nongrei village where a Brahmo prayer hall was established by a devoted Khasi Brahmo named Bardhan Roy.[19] Simiyan was an extremely generous and devoted person. "His devotion to the Almighty was increasing everyday. Many a times he used to cry at the time of offering prayers. This sense of dedication is very rare among the Khasi people. . . . Just before his death, he called all Brahmos, offered his gratitude and in folded hands bade bye to everyone and said that they would be meeting again," writes Nilmani.[20]

Nilmani made good contributions to the Khasi language. He spent more than half a century of his life in Khasi Hills and worked at the grassroots. He wrote poems, hymns, articles and essays as well as prayer books in Khasi language. In 1901, Nilmani wrote a series of articles in *The Indian Messenger* one of which, "Education in the Khasi Hills" drew attention of Sir Henry Cotton, the Chief Commissioner of Assam who asked the DPI of his province to make an enquiry and take necessary remedial steps in regards to the functioning and opening of schools in different parts of Khasi Hills. Nilmani met Henry Cotton before he left Shillong. Henry Cotton was aware of Nilmani's work but he regretted that he met Nilmani rather too late.

Working with a philanthropic zeal, Nilmani always tried to protect the interest of the local villagers on whom his influence has been immense. When H. Inglis, powerful businessman and owner of Inglis and Company[21] wanted to establish a Railway line basically to support his business of limestone and lime, that was going to affect 600 acres of orange orchard and some villages. This gentleman, H. Inglis at that time established a good network of business and for business connection he could establish a strong influence over the Khasi Chiefs and the general people of the southern Khasi Hills.[22] Because of his influence the villagers, though affected, could not take any step against Inglis. The villagers were sore about this project as they were about to be evicted from the area without the payment of any compensation.[23] It was Nilmani who took up the cause of the affected villagers and petitioned to Sir Bumflyde Fuller, the Chief Commissioner of Assam to stop this project. He argued that the Government should protect the interest of the common mass instead of protecting the interest of one wealthy individual. He argued, on behalf of the villagers, that if the railway line was allowed to pass through the area that would give a blow to the orange production of the area on which many villagers depended to earn their livelihood. The government gave due consideration to his application and the project was ultimately abandoned and the villagers were saved from being uprooted.[24] These are the pointers to the fact how Nilmani, through his selfless service to the local Khasi community earned much respect and admiration even at the highest level of the Government.

Nilmani took much interest in teaching the Khasi rural folk the modern method of agriculture and horticulture. The practice of drinking liquor was prevalent in the Khasi society. Nilmani tried to create a consciousness among the Khasis against intoxitating liquors and drugs. He took up the matter with the District administration since 1895 and suggested to stop the free trade of liquor. He wrote articles in Calcutta Press and *The Times of Assam* and submitted memorandum to the government to take steps in this regard. Even at the beginning of the twentieth century, there was no functional Excise Department in the whole of Khasi and Jaintia Hills District. That is why liquor was available everywhere freely, that was quite cheap and largely consumed by the people. Making liquor was a very common and more than fifty per cent of the houses used to prepare home made fermented liquor. Nilmani started his crusade against this evil practice and wrote to the Government seeking and suggesting remedial measures. He also wrote in this matter in *The Indian Messenger*. It was due to Nilmani's relentless efforts that the Government introduced excise duties which led to the rise of liquor prices that helped in decreasing its consumption. Further, in some areas the inter-state and inter-village traffic of liquor was now prohibited. A letter from Deputy Commissioner A.W. Dentith[25] to Nilmani Chakravarty in 1913 bears testimony of the fact: "In continuation of this office letter No. 1825 dated 8th July,1913,

I have the honour to state that Parwanas, as suggested by you, have already been issued to the Siems, Wahadadars and Sardars on the Southern and the Western parts of the Districts prohibiting an inter-state and inter-village traffic in liquor, and that the Excise Extra Assistant Commissioner has been instructed to make inquiries into working of the new Excise rules now in force during his forthcoming tour the district".[26]

In order to spread the message of ill effects of liquor and need for its prohibition, Nilmani established Khasi Hills Temperence Association at Cherrapunjee and opened its branch at Shella. This Association was affiliated to the Anglo-Indian Temperence Conference of England. Some articles about the need of prohibition in the Khasi hills also appeared in *Abkari,* the journal of the temperance Association of England. At the request of Rev. Nicholas Roy, Member of the Assam Council, Nilmani wrote some articles on the subject in *The Times of Assam* which Nicholas Roy placed before the Assam assembly while placing the Bill for introducing prohibition of liquor. At the Annual All India Temperence Conference at Calcutta in 1911, a resolution was adopted thanking the Government for taking effective steps for introducing prohibition in the Hills and to take further action. The resolution, moved by Nilmani Chakravarty, read: "... That this Conference notes with satisfaction the steps taken by the Government to prevent the spread of drinking amongst the Khonds, the Khasis and other aboriginals, but ventures to submit that further action should be taken to prevent these people being demoralized by the liquor habit".[27]

While staying at Laitkynsew, he noticed the flourishing opium cultivation in the area. Opium was being sold by the tribal villagers who carried those secretly to the foothills to sell those to the traders from Sylhet who purchased it at a very cheap rate from the tribals. Nilmani wrote an article on the ill effects of consumption of opium in *The Indian Messenger* earlier. Now, he again took up his pen and wrote to the Deputy Commissioner about the matter and pleaded for immediate remedial measures to save the Khasi people of the locality from the evils of opium consumption. Acting on Nilmani's letter, the Deputy Commissioner took immediate action and banned the cultivation or sale of opium in the area. The local people naturally got annoyed with Nilmoni and they, on an exhibition of spontaneous outburst, destroyed the Brahmo Temple that Nilmani established at Laitkynsew. The villagers, however, understood their mistake soon and reconstructed the temple within six months by providing free labour.

Very few people could assess what a great contribution was made by Nilmani Chakravarty towards the upliftment of Khasi people of the period. 'The exemplary zeal, tact, steadiness, diligence, courage and self-sacrifice with which Nilmani Chakraborty had promoted the cause of the Brahmo Samaj in the Khasi Hills for more than a quarter of a century and helped the common people in all their difficulties and led them to a higher stage of civilization than what they had occupied before 1889, is glorious indeed".[28]

The representatives of the Unitarian Church from England visited Shillong and they observed Nilmani's works for the hill people. The Unitarians, like the Brahmos, believed in the unity of God and brotherhood of man and there established a good rapport between the Brahmos and the Unitarians at Calcutta, Madras and other places. The Unitarian Church was established at Jowai by Hajom Kissor Singh Nongbri, a rebel Christian in 1887. He came to know about the Unitarian movement from Nilmani Chakravarty who referred to him to about the works of Charles Dall and his associates.[29] Soon William Ellary Channing was sent to Shillong by the Unitarian activist Charles Dall and Hellen Tompkins.[30] At Hajam Kissor Singh's invitation, Dr. Jabez Thomas Sunderland, Unitarian representative from England came to Shillong in 1896 and stayed in the house of Raj Chandra Chowdhury.[31] Later many other Unitarians worked in the hills including Anne Margaret Barr and Dr. W.H. Drummond. Hajom Kissor claimed that the Brahmos of Shillong had asked him to cooperate as Brahmos and the Unitarians had similar ideology and commitment for service and therefore gradually there established a good understanding between the Brahmos and the Unitarians. Nilmani Chakravarty, in addition to his own Brahmo Mission works, supervised the works of British and Foreign Unitarian Association at their request for nearly fifteen years at Cherrapunji and the adjoining areas. Referring to Nilmani, Spencer Lavan wrote that Brahmo Samaj had an active missionary in the Khasi Hills area and Sunderland "worked diligently to maintain his contacts with both the Brahmo Samaj and the Khasi Hills Unitarians."[32] Rev. M.C. Ratter, Representative of the Unitarians of England paid great tribute to Nilmani: "Mention is due here of the work of the Brahmo Samaj, which for years have worked in the Khasi Hills, doing a great service in its own way. Its efforts result from the untiring services of Rev. Nilmani Chakravarty. He gathered around him a number of helpers, chiefly Khasi, Many incidents proved to the people that Nilmani Chakravarty was their true friend. . . . Nilmani Chakravarty— will be remembered as one who gave his life that these primitive people might be raised up".[33]

Apart from Nilmani's efforts, the other Brahmos of Shillong also made significant contributions towards the cause of education and other related fields. An orphanage, the first orphanage exclusively for the destitute and abandoned Khasi boys was opened at *Maidan Laban* by Manmatha Nath Das Gupta in 1915. He also started a free homoeopathic charitable dispensary at Shillong.[34] In addition to establishing a number of schools, libraries and charitable dispensaries, the *Brahmo Pally* in Shillong became a hub of cultural activities. Raja Rammohan Roy Memorial meetings were held regularly every year.

Some interesting development took place in respect of inter-caste marriage which were influenced by the Brahmos. Lalmadhar Basu a Brahmo and a government official who worked at the Government Press created sensation by arranging inter-caste marriage of his two daughters.[35] He was considered the pioneer in this respect at Shillong. Brahmo influence led to widow re-marriage too. Binodini, a widow who lost her first husband during childhood, was married to Parrynath Nandy of

Kalikatchha.[36] Gurucharan Sen, another employee of the Government Press who later embraced Brahmo faith, married a girl from the orphanage at Ducca.[37] Rohini Kanta Roy, who actively supported Nilmani in his missionary work, was married to Herisa at a function at Sadharan Brahmo Samaj at Calcutta in 1910. At this wedding, which was largely attended, Bhava Sindhu Das sang Brahmo Sangeet in Khasi language. On this occasion the marriage hymns and songs were printed in Khasi language but in Bengali scripts. Many people extended their help to perform the marriage smoothly.[38] The Brahmo Samaj Annual Report of 1899 informs of two marriages performed according to Act III of 1872. Possibly that was the first ceremony of its kind. "Amongst the Khasis (it was) the first ceremony of its kind thereby laying the foundation of an advanced community.

Jeeban Roy, who has been the first Khasi Gentleman to hold a high government[39] post and later to become the Extra Assistant Commissioner, was deeply impressed and influenced by Brahmo Samaj. He made pioneering contribution towards the development of the Khasi literature. Though Jeeban Roy did not formally join the Brahmo Samaj, he came into very close contact with Nilmani and he has acknowledged Nilmani's influence in his life. He purchased a printing machine, the first by a Khasi gentleman, wrote and printed lots of books. Some of these books contained the messages of Chaitanyadeva, Gautam Buddha and the text of Ramayana. He wrote and published text books for junior classes. He also printed a few books on the ideals of Brahmo Samaj and spread that message in some villages of the hills. It was at Jeeban Roy's initiative that the Brahmos of Shillong established a middle-English school at Mawkhar Brahmo Samaj for which most of the expenditure was borne by Jeeban Roy. "He (Jeeban Roy) believed that the Bengalis are the neighbours of the Khasis and therefore Khasis must go hand in hand with the Bengalis; . . . had Jeeban Roy been surviving for a longer period, he would have contributed a lot towards his country", wrote Nilmani in his autobiography. Jeeban Roy also took the initiative to establish the first non-government English High School at

Shillong where he admitted his sons also.To preserve the socio-cultural heritage of the Khasis, the *Seng Khasi* was started by Jeeban Roy, who was indeed the apostle of Khasi renaissance.

When Ramkumar Vidyaratna visited the Khasi hills during July-August, 1884, he conducted prayers at the newly constructed house of Jeeban Roy at Shillong which was attended by 125 people.[40] Ramkumar Vidyaratna must have left a very good impression among the local population during his first visit at Shillong in 1884. He made some important suggestions to the government emphasizing the need of extending primary education to the remote villages of Khasi hills. That is why he was invited by the government to participate in the Eucation Conference of 1887 held at shillong. *The Indian Messenger* reported: Pandit Ram Kumar Vidyaratna arrived here (shillong) at the latter part of July and worked in our midst for more than three weeks. As he was invited by the Inspector of Schools to attend the Education Conference as a non-official member, much of his time was spent on conference affairs.[41] Later when Sivanath Shastri visited Shillong, he also attended a prayer at Jeebon Roy's residence.

In 1904, Brahmo Samaj got divided at Shillong. Because of some unfortunate misunderstanding among the Brahmos of Shillong a new Samaj, the Khasi Hills Brahmo Samaj, was set up by a section of Brahmos of Shillong at Laban, on a plot donated by Raj Chandra Chowdhury. Prakash Ch. Roy, father of Bidhan Chandra Roy was a frequent visitor to Shillong at that time. Dr. P.K. Roy and Chandranath Chatterjee came to Shillong around 1906 from Gaya. Three of them made an earnest initiative to bring a compromise among the dissident Brahmo Samajists of Shillong and a temporary truce was worked out.[42] And the two groups of Brahmos performed their prayers together. Since then the Khasi Hills Brahmo Samaj prayers were held in the morning and the prayers at Shillong Brahmo Mandir were held in the afternoon every Sunday.[43] There were four Brahmo Samaj prayer Halls in the town of Shillong during the Second World War, informs nonagenarian Susama Roy of Shillong.[44]

Mathuranath Nandi, a government official who worked at the Assam Secretariat came to Shillong in 1904. He was a devoted Brahmo who earned the respect of all section of the people within a short period of time. When at the intervention of Prakash Chandra Roy a compromise was arrived at among the Brahmos of Shillong, they agreed to join for prayers together with Mathuranath as *Acharya* of the Samaj. He served in that capacity for a long time. A dedicated Brahmo, Mathuranath performed his duties in right earnest. He used to speak Khasi language fluently. He recited hymns in Khasi during the prayers where the prayers were attended by Khasi people who called him *Muthulbabu.* Some Khasi gentlemen who were great admirers of Mathuranath included U.Mithi, U.Simiyan, U Sundar Ray, U Mono, U Suryamani and U Satraman. Juhari Singh and U. Scot.[45]

A true friend of the people in distress, Mathuranath established a *Ashram* (hermitage) at Laban and named it *Jogamaya Ashram*[46] where many people in distress got shelter and treatment in need. A library was also established in that *Ashram*. Mathuranath and some other inmates of the *Ashram*[47] responded to the needs of the society whenever required. When Typhoid fever spread like an epidemic in Shillong once in 1909 and again in 1911, the inmates of *Yogamaya Ashram* served the people round the clock and rendered excellent service to the community for which they received the admiration of the District administration. Mathuranath worked in the Revenue branch of the Secretariat and his main responsibility in the office was to keep the records of Immigration branch. Henry Cotton was the Chief Commissioner of Assam when Mathuranath joined the service at Shillong and several times he escorted Cotton in his trips to Calcutta. On many occasions he handed over to Henry Cotton paper cuttings of Brahmo Samaj reports of exploitation of tea garden labour which appeared in *The Indian Messenger* and other Brahmo news papers of Calcutta. A person of great honesty and integrity Mathuranath resigned from Government service later on being insulted by an European officer, N. E.

Pang. Though this officer regretted for his behaviour to Mathuranath afterwards, the latter did not compromise. Keeping his head high, Mathuranath resigned and thereafter totally dedicated himself to the cause of the common people and led an austere life at *Jogamaya Ashram* till he breathed his last in 1950.[48]

It should be mentioned that Dr. Binode Behari Roy an ardent follower of the *Naba Bidhan Brahmo Samaj*[49] opened a new Brahmo Samaj at Pomsohman locality of Cherrapunji around 1925. He was assisted in his work by one Gopal Chatterjee. In fact, some members of the Naba Bidhan Brahmo Samaj used to visit Shillong occasionally. Braja Gopal Neogi was another Naba Bidhan missionary who came to Shillong during 1920s.[50] Join Manick Singh, the Chief of Cherra, donated a plot of land near his durbar to Binode Bihari where a new Brahmo Samaj, a prayer hall and a school was established by him. Thus, the difference between the Sadharan Brahmo Samaj and the Naba Bidhan Brahmo Samaj also surfaced at remote Cherrapunji of Khasi Hills as well.

At that time regular reports of Brahmo Samaj and Brahmo Mission activities were reported in the Brahmo Newspapers of Calcutta. Sarada Manjari Dutta, an important Brahmo activist of the town wrote her biography in *Tatwa Kaumudi*. She wrote a book *Mahajatrar Pathe* which is a valuable book that depicts many activities of the Samaj at Shillong. We find some interesting news like that of the celebration that took place at Shillong after the revocation of the partition of Bengal, Jubilee celebration of the Queen at Shillong etc. in her writings. She also attended the Unitarian Conference at Allahabad and Calcutta. She also attended the annual Conference of the Mymansingh Mahila Samiti. In fact Sarada Manjari Dutta, Hemanta Kumari Chowdhury and at a later stage ladies like Subarna Prava Das, Dr. Lakshmi Prava Bora, Susama Ray, Haliman Dkhar and many others made significant contribution towards the women of the Khasi Hills. Sarda Manjari's daughter, Subarna Prava Das was the first graduate of Shillong (and second graduate of Assam). Subarna Prava took up a very successful teaching career in Shillong and made great contribution towards the cause of women's education.[51]

The Mahila Samiti established by Hemanta Kumari Devi way back in 1887 shouldered some important social responsibilities in course of time. We have mentioned earlier that its members were instrumental in opening the schools and the *Rammohan Mahila Pustakalaya* (Library). Their activities gradually extended to other fields also. Because of a number of factors during the World War the tranquil and serene atmosphere of Shillong somehow got polluted. The concentration of army, establishment of a liquor factory in Laban, teasing of girls by the soldiers—all these created some social tension. The residents of the area were of unanimous opinion that the liquor factory (brewery) was at the root of all these problem and therefore that factory be removed. When with all their best efforts the liquor factory could not be removed, the Mahila Samiti drafted a petition to the Chief Commissioner of Assam which was signed by hundreds of ladies of Shillong. Sarada Manjari Dutta and Roma Sen met Mrs. Earle, wife of the Chief Commissioner of Assam Archdale Earle and personally handed over the petition to her soliciting her good office to solve the problem. Mrs. Earle was impressed to know that there was a Ladies Club of the natives in the town and expressed her desire to visit the same. Accordingly a meeting of the Mahila Samiti was arranged at the Assam Club for the visit of the first lady of the Province. When she came, a grand reception was accorded to her. She was extremely impressed by her visit at the Samiti. In course of discussion, the members of the Samiti brought the following matters to the notice of Mrs. Earlie and prayed to exercise her good office to find out the solutions of the following:

(a) The problems that have surfaced consequent to the establishment of the brewery (liquor factory) at the civil locality of Laban.
(b) The problems being faced by the students of local Jail Road Girls' School as there is no provision to teach

English. Thus the girls were being deprived of English education.

(c) As there was only one lady doctor in the entire Shillong, the ladies were facing problems at the time of their pregnancy and during delivery of the babies. Therefore, appointment of a nursing-passed and trained mid wife as an extreme necessity to cater the needs of the Laban area.

The efforts of the Mahila Samiti bore fruits. Within a short time the brewery was removed from Laban and the Jail Road Girls' School was elevated to Middle English school. Within two months a trained nurse, holding a Diploma in nursing was appointed exclusively for the locality by the local municipality.[52]

It will be not out of place to mention that for the overall upliftment of the people of the Khasi Hills, the Brahmo Mission of Cherrapunjee, which was established by Nilmani Chakravarty, sent thirteen boys and one girl for higher education to Bengal for which the entire expenditure was borne by different Brahmo families of Bengal. The first two youth sent under this scheme were Rohinikanta Ray and Bangshabhusan. The entire responsibility and expenditure for their board, lodging and studies was borne by Bepin Behari Roy, the Zaminder of Manikdaha. Both Rohinikanto and Bangshabhusan rendered great service to the people of Khasi Hills through the Brahmo Mission. We have discussed about Rohini Kanta earlier. Bangshabhusan learnt Homoeopathy and served the poor at Cherrapunjee and the surrounding villages for a long time till his pre-mature death. A very poor young Khasi girl, who could be persuaded with great effort to go to Bengal was Heliman. She was destined to play an important role in future in the field of education and socio-cultural life of Shillong.

Heliman Dingdoh (Dhkar) was born at Cherrapunjee in 1905 in a financially weak family. Both her parents were daily wage earners. Rohini Kanta Roy initially brought this girl to the Brahmo School at Mawsisyiem along with two other Khasi girls for studies. Identifying her potentials, after much persuation, she was sent to Calcutta for higher education. Rohini Kanta and Heliman's maternal uncle escorted her to Calcutta.[53] At that time Giridih was an important centre of Brahmo activities. Along with many other humanitarian activities there, the Brahmos were running a very good school also. Heliman was sent to the Giridih School. Later she came back to Calcutta Brahmo Balika Vidyalaya from where she appeared in matriculation Examination in 1923. She passed the Matriculation Examination in first division. In fact, she ranked 9th among the first ten girls who topped the Matriculation Examination of Calcutta University that year and thus she got a scholarship of rupees twenty per month. After completing the Intermediate Arts Examination from Ducca she graduated from Bethune College Calcutta in 1923. She was later associated with Seng Khasi movement but she was totally influenced by Brahmo ideas throughout her life which she always admitted. Serving in different positions including the Head Mistress of the Jail Road High School, she was elevated to the position of Inspectress of Schools from where she superannuated in 1960s.[54] She wrote and translated a number of books in Khasi language which include the first translation of Rabindranath Tagore's drama *Chitrangada* and *Lakshmir Pariksha*. Heliman's untiring efforts and dedicated life became an ideal to the local people and she was one of the most respected figures of Shillong till she breathed her last.

The effort and dedication of the Brahmos towards the cause of higher education of women have been reflected in their initiative for the establishment of the first Women's College of the entire north-eastern region. Atulananda Das, a dedicated Brahmo functionary who was also the Deputy Chief Conservator of Forests, took serious initiative in this matter. Because of his untiring efforts (in which he received the spirited support of another like-minded person Rai Bahadur Jatindranath Chakravarty), the first Girls' College of undivided Assam—Lady Keane Girls' College—saw the light of the day in 1935. With its establishment, a long pending problem of higher education of women in the entire region was solved as till then most of the girls who wanted to pursue higher education, had to go to Calcutta as Bethune College was the nearest Girls' College for them.

When the establishment of the Girls' College at Shillong was finalized, Atulananda Das was appointed its founder Secretary and Charu Bala Datta became the President of the Governing Body. Another eminent Brahmo educationist Braja Sundar Roy became its steward. A retired Professor of City College, Calcutta and former editor of *The Indian Messenger*, Broja Sundar Roy was appointed its founder Principal. Brajo Sundar was a veteran educationist, a devoted teacher and a prolific writer. His famous book, *Aims and ideals of Indian Culture* earned high appreciation in Indian and Western academic circles. He nursed this nascent institution for five years with utmost care and devotion.[55] His scholastic attainments have made him well known and it is interesting to note that eminent personalities of Bengal like Bibhuti Bhusan Bandopadhaya (author of *Pather Panchali*), Dr. Shayama Prasad Mukherjee and Bidhan Chandra Roy came to meet Brajo Sundar in his College during their visit to Shillong.[56] It has also to be remembered that this first Girls' College of the entire north-east India, which was established at the British political head quarter of Shillong, was the only Indian college of the region till then which was established through public donations and without any government aid and therefore it was "free and more spirited than others", claims one of its alumni.[57] Chandra Nath Roy, son of Jeebon Roy was also associated with the college from its inception and served in the managing Committee in its formative stage. While laying the foundation stone of the building of the College in 1936, Lady Keane, wife of the Governor Michael Keane, highly appreciated the efforts of Atulananda Das in establishing the College and said, without him the "grooming of the college would have never been achieved."[58] Usha Bhattacharjee (1916-1981) daughter of Kamalakanta Bhattacharya served as the most successful principal of Lady Keane Girls College, Shillong for a long time and rendered yomens service towards the cause of women's higher education in the hills.

Anjali Das (later Anjali Lahiri), a Brahmo social activist rendered great service towards the upliftment of the Khasi Community particularly the women for decades.[58]

There are many other aspects of socio-cultural life of the Khasi Hills where the members of Brahmo Samaj left its mark. When the branch and the library of the Bangia Sahitya Parishad was established, Broja Sundar Roy became its first President. This library had a very good collection of rare books and manuscripts. The Brahmos of Shillong formed a literary body named *Bodhochakra* where Assamese, Bengali and Khasi gentlemen, including teachers and writers used to meet every Sunday. For the registration of Brahmo marriages in the Hills, the local administration had appointed a Brahmo missionary as a Registrar of Marriages under Act III of 1872. At the inspiration of Sabarna Prabha Chowdhury another Mahila Samiti named *Shillong Mahila Samiti* was established in 1925 at Jail Road School where all sections of the society including the poor women could join and train themselves on the art of sewing, wool stitching, making pickles and thus could start their independent profession with a small investment. Special teachers were appointed there to teach the ladies on first-aid, sewing, music and drawing.[59]

During the Second World War when the whole country faced severe crisis in respect of supply of different commodities which were rationed, the Brahmo ladies of Shillong took initiative to open *Mahila Atmarakhsha Samiti*. In addition to teach the women about the precautions to be taken by all during the War, this Samiti also started a cooperative to sale clothes at the cheapest rate at Shillong which was operating from the Jail Road School. The cooperative became so popular that soon a branch of the cooperative was also opened at Laban at the residence of Sushama Roy. Ladies themselves used to run these cooperatives, kept all accounts and issued shares. It was because of the *Mahila Atmarakha Samiti* run cooperatives, the poor and the people belonging to the middle class of Shillong got the controlled cloth all through the War period. Selling of rationed goods in the black-market, which was the most common feature during the war time elsewhere, was not felt much at Shillong. Leelamoyee Roy who served as the Head Mistress of the Bengali School, also played an important role during that period to run the *Mahila Atmaraksha Samiti*.[60]

Thus Brahmo Samaj members, though a microscopic group of people compared to the total population of Khasi and Jaintia Hills in yesteryears, could leave its mark in the local society. Their historic role in socio-cultural regeneration and in shaping the mind psyche of the people might be forgotten today but it could not be ignored historically. B. Dutta Ray opines that the future success of the Ramakrishna Mission in the Khasi Hills was due to the great missionary work earlier done by the Brahmo Samaj under Nilmani Chakravarty in the area.[61] "With the demise of Nilmani Chakravarty in 1941 Gauri Charan and Yogidhan Wahadar resurrected from the ashes of the Brahmo Samaj movement, the Ramakrishna Mission in the South Khasi Hills".[62] So much was the importance of Brahmo Samaj activities in the Khasi and Jaintia Hills that the government declared public holiday in Shillong during the *Maghotsava* festival of the Brahmos every year.[63]

B. Dutta Roy has provided some more interesting informations on the Shillong Brahmo Samaj of yesteryears: "Rai Bahadur Sadaya Charan Das, Head Assistant at the Deputy Commissioner's office who later became an Extra Assistant Commissioner was the Secretary of Shillong Brahmo Samaj at the end of the nineteenth century. His daughter Sorojini was the first woman graduate in Sylhet and was sent to England to study further. Dr. Sunderland of Unitarian Church came at that time and was a guest of Raj Chandra Choudhuri at Laban. Bramho community was a growing body in Khasi and Jaintia Hills and there were 7 branches of the Samaj with an organized Brahmo Mission. Brahmo influence was considerable. For the registration of Brahmo marriages in the hills the local administration had appointed a Brahmo missionary as a

Registrar of Marriage under Act III of 1872. Under a Government of India Resolution of 1883, Brahmo officials were allowed to absent themselves from their duties on 11 Magh, corresponding to 23-24 January in commemoration of the day on which the Brahmo Samaj was founded.... A frequent visitor who came to Shillong in 1906 was Prakash Chandra Roy, father of Dr. B.C. Roy, who lived with Dr. Mahim Chandra Choudhuri, brother of Raj Chandra Choudhuri. In 1906 Dr. P.K. Roy and Chandranath Chatterjee came from Gaya.... At that time, Manish Devi, grand-daughter of Maharshi Devendranath Tagore, and her husband Dr. Chatterjee lived at Laban. The first orphanage for Khasi boys was opened at Laban in 1915-16 at the initiative of Manmath Das Gupta. Laban became the centre of Brahmo Samaj activities with the help of Rai Bahadur Mahendra Kumar Gupta, Amar Chandra Bhattacharjee, Manmath Das Gupta and Hitendranath Nandi. On 28 January 1922 Ram Mohan Mahila Pustakalaya was opened at the Khasi Hills Brahmo Samaj Mandir at Laban. Charu Bala Sen and Jyotrimayee Gupta were Secretary and Assistant Secretary respectively. Later on Jyotirmayee became Secretary and Lilamayee Roy was Assistant Secretary, Lilamayee was the daughter of Sibnath Tatwabhusan. After sometime Sarajubala Das, Lila Roy and Santa Sen took charge of the Library.... The Centre of Khasi Brahmo Mission was transferred to Cherrapunjee in November 1890. Its Silver Jubilee was held in 1914. The Syiem of Cherra, Hajan Manick Syiem gave Nilmani Chakravarty a plot of land at Mawkisim bordering the British territory for building a school and a prayer hall, the foundation stone of which was laid in June 1892. Hali Roy was in charge of the Samaj at Cherra along with Simiyan, Shortly, sixteen centres were set up in different villages and there were 8 workers. A Committee to implement the programme of the Brahmo Samaj as decided in the Conference held in December 1892 was formed as follows:

Nilmani Chakravarty	:	President
Rai Charan Das	:	Secretary

Burdhan Roy	:	Assistant Secretary
Prakash Chandra Deb	:	Member, Shillong
Raj Chandra Deb	:	Member, Shillong
Nava Gopal Dutta	:	Member, Shillong
U Radhan Singh	:	Member, Mawkhar
U Tham Singh	:	Member, Mawkhar
Sibnath Datta	:	Member, Mawkhar
U Rushan Singh	:	Member, Nongrim
Basanta Kr. Sarma Roy	:	Member, Mawblai
U Simiyan	:	Member, Mawsmai
U Holi Singh	:	Member, Mawsmai
U Bishnu	:	Member, Laitkynsew
U Hindromoni	:	Member, Laitkynsew
U Singh Manick	:	Member, Laitkynsew
U Krishna	:	Member, Shella
U Barkrishna	:	Member, Shella
U Ba Singh	:	Member, Shella

Rohini Kanta Roy continued to conduct Brahmo prayer on Sundays at the Mawkisim Prayer Hall. He did not encounter much opposition from the organized Christian Mission. Dr. Hem Singh Wallang and Prakash Chandra continued to support him. He enjoyed the support of the simple villagers. He died in October 1941 at *"Saila Kutir"*, his Cherra home, where a Khasi lady, Balik, looked after him. With his death, the Khasi Brahmo Mission had its end. The prayer hall at Mawkisim was used only as a Primary school for some time in 1947.[64]

The Brahmo community of Khasi Hills, though a microscopic minority of about four hundred people, began to be considered a very respected group of the society at the beginning of the twentieth century. They earned this respect through their activities.

The Brahmo Samaj in Khasi and Jaintia Hills (now Meghalaya) played an important role at a certain period of its history for nearly a century. True that in Shillong it was mostly confined to the *Bengalee baboos* and a small section of the Khasi and Assamese gentlemen. However, in the southern slope of the Khasi Hills in a fifty miles radius of Cherrapunjee, it took the shape of a rural reconstruction movement under the leadership of Nilmani Chakravarty and his band of devoted Khasi Brahmo Samaj followers.

Notes and References

1. Nilmani Chakravarty, *Atmajibansmriti*, Calcutta, *Bangabda 1327*, reprint, *Bangabda 1382*, p. 74. Nilmani informs that when Devendra Nath Tagore came to know about the loan of Mowkhar Brahmo Samaj, he repaid the loan amount.
2. *The Indian Messenger*, Calcutta, 30 December, 1883.
3. *The Indian Messenger*, Calcutta, 25 November, 1883.
4. Impressed at their work great enthusiasm and conviction, Maharshi Devendra Nath Tagore donated a handsome amount of Rupees two hundred towards the construction of Bhahmo Samaj temple and used to send Rupees ten to them every month towards Brahmo Missionary work in the Khasi Hills.
5. Ajit Kumar Chakravarty, *Maharshi Devendranath Thakur*, Calcutta, 1971, p. 67
6. Nilamani Chakravarty, *Atmajibansmriti*, [First published Bangabda 1327, Calcutta], Reprint, Bangabda 1382, p. 92.
7. *The Indian Messenger*, 14 Sept., 1884. (The newspaper published a letter from Raj Chandra Chowdhury "offering some suggestion on allowing the Bangla Mahila Samaj to erect a house of their own on the Brahmo Mandir land".)
8. Sarada Manjari Dutta, *Mahajatrar Pathey*, Calcutta, Bangabda 1328, p. 58.
9. Bibhubhusan Chowdhury, Shillong: Purano diner nana katha, *SANRHITI*, Golden Jubilee Souvenir of Shillong Rabindra Smriti Granthagar, 1992, p. 75
10. This one page-leaflet was circulated by the Khasi Brahmos of Shillong and printed at the Sadharan Brahma Samaj, Calcutta.
11. Nilmani Chakravarty, *op. cit.*, p. 136.
12. Nilmani Chakravarty, *op. cit.*
13. Lakshmi Narayan Ray ed., Satis Chandra Chakravarti and Sarojendra Nath Ray compiled, *Brahmo Samaj and the Depressed Classes and Untochability*, Calcutta, 1996, pp. 41-42.
14. Sastri, History of the Brahmo Samaj, Calcutta, pp. 437-38.
15. Laksmikanta Roy ed., *op. cit.*
16. B. Dutta Roy, *Khasi Hills and the Brahmo Samaj Movement*, Proceedings of the North-East India History Association, First Session, Shillong, 1980,

pp. 138-45.

17. Sivanath Sastri, *History of the Brahmo Samaj*, First published 1912, Calcutta, Reprint, 1993, p. 319.
18. Nilmani Chakravarty, *op. cit.*
19. Nilmani Chakravarty, *op. cit.*, p. 149.
20. Nilmani Chakravarty, *op. cit.*, p. 122.
21. Assam Secretariat Reports, Revenue Proceedings A, January 1879 No. 26. Secretary to the Chief Commissioner of Assam to the Secretary, Govt. of India, Dept. of Revenue. Dt. 21 October, 1878. The report makes it clear that all a leases of the lime quarries of Khasi and Jaintia Hills were brought up by Inglis & Co.
22. W.J. Allen, *Report of the Administration of the Cosayah and Jynteeah Hills Territory*, Calcutta, 1858.
23. Nilmani Chakravarty, *op. cit.*
24. B. Dutta Ray writes: At the beginning of the century Inglis and Company owned and operated a short stretch of narrow gauge railway line—Dwara Tharia Railways, mostly to carry limestone and lime from the Khasi Hills. People from Bholaganj to Therraiaghat travelled by this line. The Inglis & Company wanted to build up a railway line with government help near Mowlang adversely affecting land and orange orchard of 600 acres without compensation. The narrow gauge line was to connect the lime quarry to a steamer station on Sylhet line and made the alignment and constructed road for railway tract. It also constructed a dam on the river on way to Shella to build a bridge over the river. This affected the trade of Shella village. The boats only could ply though the canal made for raising the embankment for the Railway. There was police to regulate the boat plying through the canal. Nilmani took up the cause of the villagers and petitioned to Sir Bamflyde Fuller, the Chief Commissioner of Assam, and A.W. Dandith, the Deputy Commissioner of the United Khasi and Jaintia Hills. Ultimately the Railway project was abandoned. *B. Dutta Roy's article in the NEIHA Proceedings, op. cit.*
25. A.W. Dentith was the Deputy Commissioner of Khasi and Jaintia Hills District. He helped Nilmani immensely in his efforts. Nilmani Chakravarty writes in his autobiography that this Deputy Commissioner promised that he would try his best to reduce the volume of liquor trade in the hills and he kept his words. Dentith also tried for the improvement of the people of the hills and helped Nilmani in his efforts.
26. Nilmani Chakravarty, *op. cit.*, p. 153
27. Nilmani Chakravarty, *op. cit.*, pp. 151-154.
28. Gautam Neogi, *A Brahmo Reformer in Meghalaya (1889-1916): A Study in the life and work of Nilmoni Chakraborty*, Proceedings of the North-East India History Association, 1989, p. 225.
29. Spencer Lavan, *Unitarians and India, a study in encounter and response*, Chicago, 1991, p. 150

30. *Ibid.*
31. Sarada Manjari Devi, *op. cit.*
32. Spencer Lavan, *op. cit.*, pp. 164-5.
33. Rev. M.C. Ratter, *To Nangroi*, Lindsey Press, London, 1932, p. 67.
34. Sarada Manjari Devi, *Mahajatrar pathe*. Manmathanath later went to Hazaribagh where he dedicated his life towards the work of Brahma Samaj and rendered great service to the community.
35. Sarada Manjari Dutta, *op. cit.*, p. 82-83.
36. B. Dutta Roy, *op. cit.*, p. 140.
37. Sarada Manjari Devi, *op. cit.*, pp. 94-95. The girl he married belonged to Dacca *Udharasram*.
38. Nilmani Chakravarty, *op. cit.*, pp. 199-200; Annual Report of Brahmo Samaj, 1899.
39. *Ibid.*, p. 140.
40. *The Indian Messenger*, 7 Sept., 1884. The news paper reported that he conducted prayers daily during his stay at Shillong and Cherrapunjee, such prayers were conducted also in the houses of Raj Chandra Achowdhury, Kailash Chandra Sen, Brajendra Nath Sen, Girish Chandra Das, Prasanna Kumar Basu, Sarat Chandra Dhar, Akshay Kr. Chatterjee, Kartick Chandra Roy of Laban, Prakash Chandra Dev and Nandiram Dass. On one occasion the prayer was held at the Beadon Falls on 19 July 1884.
41. *Ibid.*
42. *Ibid.*, p. 138.
43. *Bhakta Sadhak Mathuranath Nandi*, Sadharan Brahmo Samaj, p. 10; also Sarada Manjari Dutta, *op. cit.*, p. 132.
44. Author's interview with nonagenarian Susama Roy who resides at Laban. Smt. Roy informs that these four Brahmo Samaj temples were located at Mawkhar, Lumpering, Laban and Police Bazar.
45. *Ibid.*
46. Named after Mathuranath Nandi's wife Jogamaya Devi, who expired in 1907.
47. Some earliest inmates of the *Ashram* were Trishit Chandra Dutta, one young man named Milan, Prafulla Chandra Dutta and Atul Bhusan Sarkar.
48. *Bhakta Sadhak Mathuranath Nandi Jivani Prasanga,* Sadharan Brahmo Samaj publication, Calcutta, 1981.
49. The other faction of Brahmo Samaj at the national level who followed the teachings of Keshav Chandra Sen.
50. Diary of Late Ananth Bandhu Sen of Shillong. Part of the diary is in possession of the author (courtesy: Late Sunanda Sen). Ananth Bandhu Sen embraced Brahmo faith in 1907 and spent his life at Shillong.
51. Anjali Lahiri, *Subarna Prabha Das ebong tatkalin Nari Samaj*, Shillong 1990
52. Nilmani Chakravarty, *op. cit.*, p. 189.
53. Author's interview with Anjali Lahiri, grand daughter of Sarada Manjari Devi now octogenarian social worker and author, based at Guwahati. "To

many in the Khasi Hills, Helimandi was a living symbol of refined Brahmo spirit that touched socio-cultural life of Shillong. To us, the young students of Shillong of those days, she was like a role model—we all tried to follow her", says Anjali Lahiri, who was in close contact with Heliman since her childhood. Anjali Lahiri, in course of discussion with the author have thrown light on an unexplored aspect of Heliman's life—her participation in the national movement. Heliman started her teaching career at Ducca Eden School. There she was much influenced by Mukundadas, Sushil Bose, Aurobindo Ghosh and other revolutionaries with whom she had personal contacts. They requested Heliman to perform a courageous act. She was given Rs.4,000 by them to hand-over the same to a revolutionary who was detained at Ducca jail and for this she was to go to the jail on the disguise of a *sanyasini* named *Mukti Maa*. She agreed to do the same but then somehow the whole plan was leaked out. She was immediately suspended from her job as the school where she was serving was a government School. Further her movement came under the scrutiny of the CID. It was because of this fact Heliman fled from Ducca to Shillong where she settled down finally.

54. Golden Jubilee Souvenir, Lady Keane Girls' College, Shillong, 1986.
55. Author's interview with Indira Khusalini, daughter of Broja Sundar Roy in 1984 when she was residing at 48 Park Street, Calcutta. Indira Devi passed her Bachelor of Arts Examination from Lady Keane Girls' College
56. Golden Jubilee Souvenir, *op. cit.*, article by Kapila Chatterjee.
57. *Ibid.*
58. Extract from the speech delivered by Lady Keane at the foundation Laying ceremony of the College on 25 July 1936. Golden Jubilee Souvenir, *op. cit.* See Press clippings. It may be mentioned here that Atulananda was the uncle of famous poet, Jibanadanda Das.
59. Anjali Lahiri, *op. cit.*, p. 67.
60. Author's interview with nonagenarian Susama Roy at Shillong, who is residing at Laban, Shillong; Also, Anjali Lahiri, *op. cit.*, p. 68.
61. B. Dutta Ray, NEIHA Proceedings, *op. cit.*, p. 143.
62. B. Datta Roy, *History of Shillong 1864-1947*, The Shillong Times Golden Jubilee Souvenir, Shillong, 1995, p. 21
63. Home (A) Proceedings of Chief Commissioner of Assam, No. 32-52. February 1902, cited in B. Dutta Ray, *Assam Secretariat 1874-1947: An Administrative History of North-East India,* Shillong.
64. B. Dutta Ray, NEIHA Proceedings, *op. cit.*

3

BRAHMO SAMAJ AND THE PLANTATION WORKERS IN ASSAM

Brahmo Samaj in India has the unique distinction of being the first organization to give attention to the inhumane suffering of the tea garden workers of Assam in the nineteenth century. To understand the historic role played by Brahmo Samaj, we would attempt to throw some light on the background that paved the way for this exploitation of the tea gardens workers.

Tea was discovered in wild condition in upper Assam by two brothers—Alexander Bruce and Robert Bruce. The cultivation of tea was introduced in Assam by the East India Company in the third decade of the nineteenth century when experimental tea garden was introduced in upper Assam. Though tea was first successfully manufactured in 1937, initial efforts of the Company for commercial production of tea did not bear much fruit. However, the situation changed soon and tea cultivation started in full scale during the middle of the nineteenth century when, consequent to abolition of East India Company's monopoly of trade, private capital began to be invested in the trade. The Assam Company, the first joint stock Company of India started tea cultivation in right earnest in 1939 and for the next one and a half decade they virtually retained the monopoly of tea cultivation in Assam. Soon other European Companies were floated and by 1870-71 a massive area of 6,25,780 acres were allotted to the planters at a very concessional rate by the colonial administration[1] which gave birth to a new form of economic exploitation under the Planter Raj.

What followed in the gardens was an unheard form of exploitation. Even at the cost of repetition, the story of untold suffering of the plantation workers, who were popularly known as *Coolies*, need to be narrated in some details. For their own survival at that nascent stage, the plantation economy needed cheap labour and the planters tried all possible ways to recruit local labour. However, the wage offered by the Company failed to attract local labour, who were by nature also, apathetic to work. Therefore, by 1860 labour began to be recruited from outside the province and within a decade more than two-thirds of the labour in the plantations of Assam migrated from outside. Lakhs of agricultural labourers rendered surplus by the decaying agrarian economy in different parts of India, particularly from the then Central Provinces and the United Provinces, formed the source of supply of labour force for tea plantations in Assam. The main agents of these recruits were the *Arkanthis* and the *Sardars* and through them started the crudest form of exploitation of the working class population in the recorded history of India.

The *Arkanthis* were the managing agents or contractors for labour supply who used to work on a commission. These contractors tried their best to supply labour but the method of recruitment and the way these people were sent to Assam were inhuman. "During the period of two years from 15 December 1859 to 21 November 1861 the Assam Company brought 2,272 recruits from outside of whom 250 or 11 per cent died on the way. Of a total of 2,569 recruits who were sent down Brahmaputra in two batches during the period from 2 April, 1861 to 25 February, 1862, as many as 135 died or got drowned and 103 absconded. Of 84,915 recruits from Assam between 1 May, 1863 and 1 May, 1866, 30,000 died by 30 June, 1866. Based on different reports, S.K. Bose showed how in the Bamuni Tea Estate of Nowgaon 62 out of 150 coolies employed died in six-month period during the year 1865 (the percentage of death being 41.3 per cent).[2] Such high mortality of immigrant labour did cost the planters. For the price charged by contractors per recruit ranged from Rs.12 to Rs.20. "Men, women and children were enticed, even kidnapped, and traded like cattle; absconders were hunted down like runaway slaves", observes Amalendu Guha.[3] The *Sardar* or the foreman of the garden also became a recruiting agent—he secured labourers through numerous local channels and agents. The method they followed in labour recruitment was almost as fraudulent as that prevailed with recruitment of outside labourers. In 1957, a tea garden labourer could earn in real wages about Rs.2 and Annas 8 per month. Still, with the extension of the plantations, the total number of workers in tea industry went on increasing and towards the end of the nineteenth century over six lakhs people were working in tea gardens. Because of their condition of abject poverty, the unfortunate rural mass fell into the clutches of the unscrupulous recruiting agents.

The plantations being the virtual monopoly of the British capitalists, these destitute rural mass who now got the new status of *coolie* in Government records, became an easy prey to the planters' lust. "No moral scruple deterred them from or their *Sirdars* in resorting to all sorts of heinous methods in securing, torturing and exploiting the labourers—whether male, female or tender aged child. The most sorry part of it is that this occurred with the veiled and sometime unveiled connivance of the colonial administration itself. For instance, the British planters considered securing groups of married couple more profitable than securing unrelated men and women. The *Sirdars* at once secured through reckless dupery and coercive intoxication such men and women and forced them to live as couple who were not at all wedded pairs. Thus secured and virtually kept imprisoned in the tea gardens, these unfortunate labourers had to undergo untold miseries. The barbarities perpetrated upon them were conceivable only in a colonial regime", writes Sukomal Sen.[4] The life of the plantation workers became so hazardous and painful not only in terms of low wages but in respect of housing, sanitation, food-supply and the cruelty meted to them by the planters. Physical torture, flogging and caning of the coolies—irrespective of men, women and children by the planters were very common. Malnutrition and disease, working upon an originally fragile health quite incapacitated many coolies and on many occasions they had to embrace death. Abduction of married women, unlawful engagement of children of even five years of age, fraud, wrongful confinement, intimidation—all these became an integral part of the Planter Raj and had its spiral effect—many died in the very first year of their arrival in Assam. And it is because of their high mortality rate coupled with desertions and inadecquacy of local recruit in the tea gardens, indentured labour had to be brought continually from other parts of India to Assam.

Often the planters' cruelty resulted fatally. But the workers were denied justice as the planters had a close nexus with the colonial administration. How even the fatal death of a coolie caused by merciless flogging of the planter was defended by the local administration could be evidenced from an official report of 1866-7. Candidly blaming the climate of Assam for the death of the coolies the Commissioner of upper Assam reported: "In Assam the life of a coolie hangs at best by a slender thread; with a climate that so saps his vitality, it virtually takes very little to kill him; and the shock of such a flogging as would be elsewhere borne with impunity might there prove fatal."[5]

However, some later British civil servants, though microscopic in number, gradually understood the gravity of the situation. Sir George Campbell described that the coolie recruitment system reduced the position of the coolies to that of slave. Sir Bampfylde Fuller termed the condition of the coolies as that of "beasts in a menagerie". In his biography, *Some Personal Experiences*, Fuller gives a vivid account of how a coolie was flogged to death by the garden's European assistant officer. When the case was filed in the lower court, the officer was sentenced to eighteen months' simple imprisonment. But that created much agitation among the planters who now defended the officer by all possible means. The case was referred to the High Court which acquitted the officer under the pressure of

European agitation.[6] Among the British civil servants Henry Cotton remains an honourable exception who tried honestly to improve the workers' living condition and increase their wages while in office with true philanthropic zeal, but he had to resign from service for his earnest endeavour. But being clear to his conscience and a believer in England's civilizing mission of India, Henry Cotton carried on his persistent campaign against the Planter Raj ever since. But not much change could be effected in the system. Cotton's autobiography gives vivid account of this semi-feudal system of exploitation by the Planters.[7] "... In some instances only a few annas (or pence) found their way into the hands of a coolie as wages in the course of the whole year...."[8] observed Henry Cotton.

These plantation workers became the victims of the crudest form of capitalist exploitation. By 1860s, the European capital and labour from different parts of India began to emigrate to Assam and settle down in the Tea Estates. By the turn of the century, this immigrant labour force, numbering 645,100, constituted nearly eighty-three per cent of the total tea garden workers of Assam.[9] These workers, who by 1900 constituted nearly nine per cent of the total population of the province, were the most exploited people as they remained far away from their native places and were dumped in an altogether new environment which practically snatched away from them all sorts of bargaining power.[10] The pathetic and inhuman condition in which these plantation workers passed their days are well known. "The coolies were in a state of quasi-slavery, no state of recognized slavery could be worse", stated Surendranath Banerjee in his memorandum to the Government in 1888.[11] Referring to the situation, Bipan Chandra observed, "Thus began the tale of woe and misery of the Assam tea-plantation labourers who found to their sorrow that the 'economic development' of the country by foreign capitalists, while resulting in the creation of new opportunities of employment, threw them from the frying pan of their traditional rural poverty into the fire of misery and exploitation of indentured labour."[12]

The pathetic condition of the coolies were reported in contemporary Bengal newspapers—particularly *Dacca Prakash*, *Somprakash* and *Sanjibani*. One of the earliest reports in relation to the coolies of Assam gardens that could be traced in *Somprakash*, which published a long report based on the reports of *Dacca Prakash*.[13] "For some time different newspapers had been agitating upon the oppressions committed by the tea planters of Cachhar. Then the tea planters took a conciliatory attitude. But now again with the gradual passage of time they are becoming arrogant. . . . Earlier the planters paid Rs.2 and Annas 8 to the labourers of tea gardens as monthly wage. . . . Is it not oppression? . . . We hereby warn the tea planters again not to behave like indigo planters. If they continue oppressions like that of indigo planters, they shall have to leave India soon."[14]

The attention of the Brahmo Samajists were drawn to the problems of tea garden workers of Assam around the same time. From 1860s they played a very positive role in mobilizing public opinion for emancipation of these workers who were ipso-facto treated as serfs by the European planters. As stated earlier, by 1860s, the European capital and labour from different parts of India firmly settled down in the Tea Estates and with this settlement was related the woeful story of suffering humanity in colonial India. Members of Brahmo Samaj fraternity, most of whom were products of the new spirit of enquiry and free thinking fed by rationalism and progressive ideas, naturally came forward to mobilize public opinion in favour of the oppressed coolies in the remote tea gardens of Assam.

In the general framework of their social reform programme during the second half of the nineteenth century, the Brahmo Samaj activists of Bengal began to discuss the problems of the Assam *coolies*[15] in their regular meetings. Gradually understanding the magnitude of the problem and being sympathetic to the tea garden workers' abject condition of virtual serfdom, the Brahmo Samajists decided to mobilise public opinion against the most crude capitalist exploitation of the Planter Raj. Imbued with philanthropic orientation, a group of dedicated Brahmos championed the cause of the tea garden workers of Assam. This group of people who volunteered to come forward for the emancipation of tea garden labourers included Sibnath Sashtri, Ganesh Chandra Ghosh, Heramba Chandra Maitreo, Kalisankar Sukul, Ramakumar Bhattacharjee (Vidyaratna) etc., and they were led by Dwaraka Nath Ganguli.

Ramakumar Bhattacharjee (Vidyaratna), who came to Assam as an emissary of the Brahmo Samaj during 1879-80, deserve the most gracious credit of bringing the whole matter of exploitation of the tea garden workers to the notice of the general public of Bengal and Brahmo Samaj activists of Bengal in particular. During his tour of Assam, Ramkumar visited a number of tea gardens at high risk (and sometimes in the disguise of a coolie) to gather first hand information about the life of the tea garden workers. Though one of the missions of Ramkumar's visit to the province included preaching of Brahmo faith, he could attract only a microscopic section of the Assamese society. This failure was however, compensated by his successful endeavour to mobilize public opinion in Bengal towards the cause of emancipation of tea garden workers, which he did in the spirit of a true social reformer. In 1880 Ramkumar Vidyaratna wrote a book named *Udashin Satyasrabar Assam Bhraman* in which he gave vivid description of the life in the tea gardens in Assam which reminded the readers about *Uncle Tom's Cabin.*[16] It is a thought provoking book in which the writer along with a descriptive account of the white planters' oppression of the coolies tried to focus the economic consequences of the introduction of the Planter Raj in Assam. In this book Ramkumar stated that while the white planters derived huge profit from the tea cultivation, the working class, the plantation labour, who were the chief factor of production, practically got no benefit from this profit compared to their hard work. Further, the planters practically have made no contribution towards the economic upliftment of the province of Assam while they are becoming multimillionaires by exploiting its natural resources. *Udashin Satyasrabar Assam Bhraman* was the first ever sincere effort of documentation of the happenings in the tea gardens in Assam on the basis of one's own first hand practical experience.

In 1888, Ramkumar's famous book *Coolie Kahini* was published. This book, containing twenty-six chapters, gives a vivid and analytical description of the tea garden life of Assam as it was in the second half of the Nineteenth century. How women coolies were compelled to become the victims of the planter's lust, the close link of the planters with the government machinery, the role of the *Arkanthis*, the corrupt inhuman practice of the coolie recruits—all have been very authentically portrayed in Ramkumar's writings. Ramkumar also gave some interesting information about tea garden administration. For example, Ramkumar wrote that some of the gardens had their own secret prisons where they used to keep the run away labour when they were recaptured. Based on true facts gathered on the author's first hand information, the language of *Coolie Kahini* is very lucid which makes the book an interesting and touchy reading. On the whole, *Coolie Kahini* is excellent and faithful portrayal of the life in the tea gardens of Assam as it was in the last quarter of the nineteenth century.[17]

All these writings and contemporary publication in the newspapers, mostly owned by the Brahmos, have been instrumental in mobilizing public opinion against the crude capitalist exploitation which were being carried out by the white planters of the tea estates in Assam. There should be no hesitation to recognize the historic role played by the Brahmo Samajists in this regard. Biswanath Mukhopadhaya observed, "Till then the cry of the tea gardens of Assam reached nobody crossing the hills. Ramkumar was the first person who began to publish all these news in *Sanjibanee*. The people of Bengal started trembling in shock after reading these news of inhuman oppression."[18]

In 1886, Dwarka Nath Ganguli, a dedicated Brahmo social reformer, came to Assam as an emissary of the Indian Association to acquire a first hand knowledge about the prevailing condition of the plantation workers of the province. Sivanath Sastri, the Head of the Sadharan Brahmo Samaj at Calcutta also visited Assam around the same time. Both of them, particularly Dwarka Nath, were instrumental in bringing the plantation workers' problem to the All India political platform in future. Dwarka Nath Ganguli was also associated with *Sanjibani* at that time. Regarding his Assam visit Sivanath Sastri writes, "... Once he (Dwarka Nath Ganguli) personally visited the tea estates of Assam to get acquainted with the living condition of the tea plantation workers. It was a rainy session., the Brahmaputra flooded its two banks, the communication network had broken down. He paid no heed to the repeated requests made to him by different quarters to cancel his journey to Assam at that time. In spite of the inclement weather and flood, he continued his mission. During his journey, once he fell into the river and was swept away by the current of the river. On that day he narrowly escaped. Yet there was no dearth of enthusiasm for the task for which he came to Assam. His visit created a serious problem for the British officials of the province. What for Dwarka Nath Ganguli, Asst. Secretary of the Indian Association has come to Assam? That posed a very big question to the British official circle in Assam and they became extremely cautious and alert. Wherever he went police followed him. At many places the Deputy Commissioners began to collect news about the purpose of his Assam visit from the local Bengali families. However in the face of these heavy odds, Dwarka Nath's mission became very much successful. He collected a lot of information about the functioning of plantation and the life of its workers, which he began to despatch for publication in *Sanjibani*."[19] Sivanath Sastri also left an interesting description of how he and Dwarka Nath Ganguli were subjected to strict surveillance by the local administration during their visit to Assam in 1886 and how the planters and the local administration took steps to prevent their entry in the tea gardens.

How much cautious and apprehensive the local administration became during the visits of these Brahmo social reformers in the Brahmaputra valley could be evidenced from the fact in some cases the Deputy Commissioners themselves were keeping vigil over them. Narrating his Dibrugarh experience where he was supposed to attend a meeting and deliver a lecture, Sastri writes, "While most of the local residents and gentlemen could not attend the meeting because of inclement weather, the Deputy Commissioner was present. Wherever I addressed the meetings and wherever I went, the English officials enquired from the local gentlemen and advocates: Who is Sivanath Sastri? . . . Has he come here with the politically motivated intension to enquire the condition of tea garden coolies?"[20] His dispatches and articles (sometimes published under the pen name, *Son of Lengi*) were published serially during the period in the Calcutta newspapers, both English and Bengali, which came as a rude shock to the educated intelligentsia of Bengal.[21]

The visit of Dwarka Nath to Assam resulted in mobilizing public opinion in Bengal in favour of the tea garden coolies. On his return from Assam, he wrote a series of articles in different newspapers, particularly in *Sanjibani*, thus arousing the latent nationalism of the readers with real-life first hand description and the hair-raising stories of atrocities that were meted to the tea garden coolies by their planter masters.[22] A collection of thirteen such articles are now available and those show the pain and hard labour that Dwarka Nath undertook to bring the distressing plight of the coolies to the notice of the public.[23] Dwarka Nath's similar writings also appeared in the *Bengalee*, *Tatwabodhini Patrika* and the *Brahmo Public Opinion* which include articles titled "ignorant and timid coolies" and "Child life in tea gardens".

It is difficult to say how much impact the visit of these two Brahmo activists—Dwarka Nath and Sivanath—had on the local working class population because they did not get the opportunity to address the tea garden labourer anywhere in Assam. But they addressed meetings of Brahmo Samaj at Nagaon, Tezpur, Dibrugarh, Sibsagar and other places. What impact they had in shaping the mindset of the coolies during the period could not be ascertained as no data is available but there might be some co-relation in the increase of the court cases that have been filed by the plantation workers of different gardens against their masters on different issues during post-1886 period.

The problem of tea garden coolies failed to attract much attention of the newly emerging Assamese intelligentsia and the middle class in Assam due to a number of reasons. One reason was that some of the newly educated people did not want to come into conflict with the European planters as any such move would have been construed as anti-government as the planter-provincial government nexus was very strong. Secondly, some members of the slowly emerging middle class themselves joined the plantation business in due course of time. Except for a microscopic few like Laksminath Bezbaruah the response of the mass towards the burning problem of coolies was one of apathy. Prasenjit Chowdhury has dealt these aspects in his study, *Asomar Chah Banua aru Unoish Satikar Vidyat Samaj*. Chowdhury points out how persons like Padmanath Gohain Baruah, who were not otherwise known to be sympathetic about the problems of the working class, were touched by the activities and writings of Brahmo philanthropists like Krishnakumar Mitra. Gohain Baruah included a short biography of Krishnakumar in his book *Nitikatha*, which was written as a textbook for the school children. Gohain Baruah wrote: "Late Krishnakumar Mitra was a selfless patriot and deeply religious man. Through *Sanjibani*, a paper which was run and edited by him, the bad luck of the tea garden coolies of Assam were slightly changed. Therefore, to show respect to him I am incorporating a short biography of late Krishna Chandra Mitra in my *Nitikatha*."[24]

Lakhsminath Bezbaruah was initiated to Brahmo faith. His great contribution towards Assamese literature earned him the title *Sahitya-rathi*. He was indeed the pioneer among the Assamese gentleman to take up the cause of tea garden labour and to defend them through his writings. His debate on the issue with Boli Narayan Bora in the pages of *Mou* generated much interest. When Boli Narayan, the Editor of the Assamese journal *Mou* (published from Calcutta), brought out several articles criticizing the labour-friendly attitude of the Brahmo Samaj activists in Bengal, supporting the European planters on the indentured coolie question and portraying a rosy picture of the tea garden coolies in Assam, Lakhsminath Bezbaruah made spirited protests. In fact, the newly educated Assamese students of Calcutta never supported *Mou's* stand and Bezbaruah became their spokesman. Bezbaruah wrote in the pages of *Mou*: "On being touched and pained at the plight of the tea garden coolies some patriotic Bengali gentlemen are trying their best to mobilize public opinion to redress their grievances. I do not know why disturbance is being created by you in this matter and you have started them criticizing left and right without going into the root cause of suffering (of tea garden coolies) and how far your stand is justified." On another occasion Bezbaruah wrote, "We do not agree with your view that coolies die because of their laziness which deprive them of their salary. Those people who have come from the distant parts of India to serve in the plantations under unbearable threat and harassment—why should they be lazy and why should they die of laziness after coming to an alien country (Assam)—who would be going to solve that puzzle!"[25]

Bezbaruah and Gohain Baruah's observations however were isolated instances, it does not necessarily reflect the sentiment of the mass or the slowly emerging middle class of Assam, who were generally apathetic towards the problem. Another Brahmo gentleman Kamalakanta Bhattacharya was touched at the silence of the Assamese people on the issue. In one of his writings in the *Assam Bandhu* he lamented, ". . . shame with us, the residents of Assam. We have become outsiders in our own house today. The Planters have become zaminders—he has accumulated all the wealth and respects. Shame we, the Assamese people, for we have very weak hearts".[26] In contemporary Bengal, however, there was some sympathy towards the oppressed tea garden workers of Assam, even among the contemporary middle class.

It is worth mentioning that at that point of time a number

of other publications also came out in Bengal which were based on the life of tea garden workers of Bengal. A drama, *Chah Kar Darpan* which was written in the line of *Nil Darpan* by Dakshina Ranjan Chattopadhaya and published in 1875 from Calcutta deals with the oppression of the tea garden workers by the planters. The unique feature of the book is that it carries a litho picture in its title cover which portrays how a coolie girl was oppressed by a white planter.[27]

Another novel named *Chah Coolir Atmakahini* was written by Jogendranath Chattopadhaya, the noted novelist of the nineteenth century Bengal. We get reference to yet another drama on tea garden life in Assam written by one Prasannalal Mukhopadhaya and published from Calcutta in 1875.[28] However, Ramkumar Vidyaratna's *Udashin Satyasrabar Assam Bhraman* has more historical value as it was based on the writer's personal experience. It need to be mentioned that another book titled *Assam Bhraman* was also written around the same time by an unknown Brahmo missionary which was also published from Calcutta in 1889. The author gives a vivid description of coolie life in gardens, including the fate of the runaway slaves in the "discipline houses" (the temporary jails established in the gardens by the planters). The unknown author of the book writes, "Words fall short to write about the oppression that continues in the Tea gardens. You are a coolie—you have got some disease—that does not matter, you shall have to go to work. If you do not go, the hunter in my hand will eat out the flesh of your back. You are weak, can't work, that does not mean anything. Unless you can dig thirty *nal* of land, you will not get your wage."[29]

Lord Ripon's energetic reform measures inspired the Brahmo Samajists to bring the Assam coolie problem to his notice with the hope that his personal intervention might bear some positive results in this respect. Meanwhile, in 1876 at the initiative of Surendranath Banerjee and Ananda Mohan Bose the Indian Association (*Bharat Sabha*) was formed and a substantial number of Brahmos became active members amongst whom were included Dwarkanath Ganguly (who also became its Assistant Secretary), Sivanath Sastri and Ramkumar Vidyaratna. The aims and objectives of the Association, in the words of Surendranath Banerjee, were to make it the centre for the national movement of resurgent India, to develop strong public opinion, to unite the people of India belonging to diverse races and religion and to protect the interest of all section of the Indians.[30] Majority of the members and most of the office bearers of the Indian Association were Brahmos at the nascent stage of the Indian Association. Bipin Chandra Pal observes, "... The Indian Association received material assistance from the leaders of Sadharan Brahmo Samaj, almost all of whom were members of the Executive Committee of the Indian Association."[31]

It was because of the initiative taken by the members of the Brahmo Samaj that the problems of Assam plantation workers became a regular matter of discussion at the meetings of the Indian Association. Soon the Indian Association became the spokesman of the rising generation of young nationalists. The Government introduced the Inland Emigration Bill in 1881 (which became an Act in 1882). In 1881, immediately after the introduction of the Bill, the Indian Association submitted a detailed memorandum to the Government of India vehemently criticizing certain provisions, particularly Sections 170 and 172 of the Bill. When the memorial was submitted to Lord Ripon, a copy of Ramkumar's book (*Udashin Satya-srabar Assam Bhraman*) highlighting the inhuman practice of coolie recruits, the role of *Arkanthis* (recruiters) was also attached and they urged upon Lord Ripon to intervene. Lord Ripon referred to this book and the memorandum in his speech when the Inland Emigration Bill was being discussed in the Bengal Council on 5 January, 1882. Lord Ripon instructed the Chief Commissioner of Assam to look into the matter. In spite of the fact that Lord Ripon gave specific assurance to the Indian Association delegates that the Government's attention was being drawn towards this matter and steps would be taken in near future to ameliorate the grievances of the coolies and there would be changes in the method of coolie recruitment,[32] nothing concrete materialized. The Act of 1882 when passed, was condemned by the nationalists through out the country as "Slave-law".

However the members of The Brahmo samaj as well as the Indian Association continued their efforts. In 1886, the Association gave a memorial to the Viceroy again inviting his personal intervention in matters related to Assam coolies. The members of the Indian Association and Brahmo Samaj also drew the attention of the British Government through the Secretary of States for India towards the matter. Due to their persistent efforts, the Secretary of States for India directed that the working of the Act should be "narrowly watched" and assured that the law might not be continued in practice.[33] After Dwaraka Nath's Assam visit the number of labour related cases in the courts of Assam increased considerably but judgments of the court almost always went in favour of the planters. The Indian Association brought this to the notice of the Government of India through another memorial which was submitted on 5 May, 1888. That bore no fruit. Still the Association continued its efforts and kept on sending memorials year after year.[34] The frustration of Indian Association members on the failure of Government to take effective steps on emancipation of tea garden workers could be evidenced from the following lines of the Report of the Indian Association: "The worst anticipation of those who objected to the enactment of Coolie Act of 1882 had been more than realized. No action had been taken in spite of persistent disclosures of newspapers, which revealed a ghastly tale of horror and a condition of things which practically amounted to a species of slavery, thriving under the protection of British laws and sanctioned by British Government".[35] Echoing the same feeling the *Brahmo Public Opinion* also published a long editorial commenting how the British intellectuals who were championing the cause of democracy, failed to oppose the newly introduced slave laws being executed by the government.[36]

Some of the news items regarding the oppression in the tea gardens of Assam created sensations not only among the educated intelligentsia of Bengal but also among the mass. Particularly two judicial mockeries, one case related to Mr. Webb (who was acquitted by the Court though he killed a coolie girl) and the other in regard to killing of a minor tea garden worker, Umesh, (Umesh murder case) when published in these news papers, led to serious public debate. These articles were also translated into English and published in the *Race and Ryots*, an English newspaper which unmasked the real face of the planters.[37] All these perturbed the planters very much. Being alarmed, the planters began to declare openly that "The contributor to *Sanjibanee* will be the first victim of the planter's gun."[38] At this stage Ramkumar's movements had to be restricted because attempts were being made to even kill him as he collected a number of documents with the proof of forgery of some planters. He sent these documents to the Chief Commissioner of Assam for his perusal. "At that time Ramkumar had to be very careful. Because at every moment attempts were made to kill him. He collected some forged documents and account of the planter to the Chief Commissioner."[39]

This group of Brahmo Samajists also wanted to bring the Webb issue to the notice of the general public of Bengal and with that aim in view printed a memorandum titled *Justice murdered in India: The papers of the Webb Case regarding the sacrifice of a daughter of India to the lust of an Anglo-Indian.* The pamphlet, prepared by a group of energetic Brahmos were distributed through the Indian Association. It is worth mentioning here that the Brahmo Samajists, along with mobilizing public opinion in Bengal also adopted a good strategy to bring the matter to the notice of the members of the British Parliament. Till then, the Brahmos and for that effect the members of the Indian Association had faith in the British civilizing mission and therefore the booklet was dedicated to the "Electors of Great Britain and Ireland." The papers of the Webb case regarding "sacrifice of daughter of India to the lust of an Anglo-Indian" (in this case a coolie girl was raped and later murdered by an European Officer) was sent for tabling in the British

Parliament through Mr. William Squans, a member of the British Parliament.[40]

The Webb case and the Umesh Murder case were published serially during the period in Brahmo and other newspapers, both English and Bengali. These news gave a rude shock to the educated intelligentsia of Bengal.[41] It needs to be mentioned that during the same period the court cases in relation to the plantation workers began to increase though the European planters became more and more defensive on the issue.[42] Some Brahmos made monetary contribution towards the cost of litigation. Devendra Nath Tagore contributed Rupees one hundred in 1893 as assistance towards "fighting a court case related to death in Assam."[43] On several occasions funds were raised and old clothes were collected for providing relief to the tea garden workers at the initiative of some Brahmo activists. Atul Chandra Roy, a Brahmo doctor stationed at Dhubri distributed such relief to many immigrant labourers when they passed through Dhubri steamer ghat where all ships carrying tea garden labour from the up country used to stop for health check up of the coolies. Most of these labourers were the catch of the *Arkanthis* or recruiting agents who attracted them by giving them the rosy picture of handsome remuneration in the tea districts of Assam. By the time they reached Dhubri "many died and hundreds were half dead."[44]

Apart from the infamous cases of Webb, Francis and Umesh—which were made public by the efforts of the Brahmo Samaj activists through Brahmo newspapers, some other sensational cases of coolie oppression in which the planters were involved were also recorded in the *Indian Messenger*. Publishing three such cases—that of Driberg, Byrne and that of an European Manager—the newspaper observed that was the time for the Supreme Government to direct their attention to the unfortunate province of Assam. The newspaper reported: "Assam has of late been drawing considerable public attention from the large number of cases of brutal assaults committed by the planters on helpless natives. The notorious cases of Francis and Webb have scarcely been forgotten by the public when they have startled afresh by the reports of two more cases—one of Driberg, a Railway driver and the other of Byrne.... The former was sent up for trial before the Asst. Commissioner of Debrugar on a charge of 'using criminal force towards a woman with intent to outrage her modesty'—and has been sentenced to one month's simple imprisonment and to pay a fine of Rs.200—by no means an adequate punishment for such a heinous offence.... The second case refers to the death of a native mahut whom Byrne took for a wild beast and shot dead.... Some means should be found to check this growing evil.... The *Sanjibani* publishes another outrageous story from Assam, which relates to the misdeeds of a Planter—the Manager of a tea garden—and the indifference of the local authorities to give protection to the unfortunate coolly the honour and virtue whose young daughter was on peril. If all those stories are true, then surely it is high time for supreme government to direct their attention to this unfortunate province."[45]

Brahmo Samaj literature, (books, newspapers, booklets etc.) have been instrumental in mobilizing public opinion against the crude capitalist exploitation which were being carried out by the white Planters of the tea estates in Assam. How was the middle class reaction to these writings in Bengal? After reading Ramkumar's *Coolie Kahini* and other articles, Jaladhar Sen, the celebrated author of the nineteenth century Bengal wrote: "when we used to read his articles about the tales of coolies in Assam in the newspapers—the way he dared to do some work risking his life—reading those description we used to offer flowers to him in gratitude."

The role played by the Brahmo newspapers in arousing latent nationalism of the readers by depicting the fate of the oppressed tea garden workers cannot be overestimated. The Samaj and the Indian Association were undoubtedly two most important forums of the late nineteenth century India and both attracted much attention of the Indian intelligentsia throughout the country. When these two bodies started continuous campaign on the tea garden coolie exploitation, others nationalist forums understood the gravity of the issue of coolie exploitation. Particularly in 1881 public were shocked, when the draconian Emigration Bill was tabled in the Bengal Council. That is why we see that after the formation of the Indian Association there was a sudden consciousness throughout India about the fate of the tea garden coolies. *The Indian Spectator*, published from far off Bombay opposed the legislation and commented that the Act was "nothing short of legalized thralldom for the unhappy Bengali coolly. . . . Never was labour left so entirely at the mercy of the capital".[46] For the first time an issue related to Assam received so much of attention by the national media as well as the intellectuals of the country. So long such consciousness was related to Bengal only. Bipan Chandra cites the name of number of newspapers that brought out reports and editorials on the issue; these include *Aftab-i-Hind, Prabhati, Hindu, Bharat Mihir, Sahachar, Ananda Bazar Patrika, Mahratta, Kesari, Hitavadi, Tribune, Rahbar, Kaiser-i-Hind, Voice of India*, etc.[47] It goes without saying that this national consciousness on the issue was possible because of the untiring efforts of the members of the Indian Association members, most of whom belonged to the Brahmo fraternity in 1880s. Rightly commented David Kopf that Brahmo Samaj was the real torch bearers of bringing changes in the attitude and mindset of the people of India. Its members who formed the Indian Association "represented a new generalized political consciousness in India, which went beyond begging or petitioning favours from the Queen but felt short of a direct confrontation with the British authority and declaration of independence."[48]

As discussed earlier, the problems of the immigrant tea garden workers in Assam who were living in a state of quasi slavery, as termed by Surendranath Banerjee, was an important agenda of Brahmo Samaj activities at many places towards the end of the nineteenth century. Not only the enlightened Brahmos of Calcutta discussed the subjects in its meetings, in true philanthropic zeal they could succeed in spreading the message to smaller towns of Bengal as well. We get references that Brahmo volunteers visiting the railway station at Nalhati to prevent the newly recruited coolies from going to Assam. Referring to the Brahmo activists of Nalhati in the Birbhum district of Bengal, Sivanath Sastri writes, "They organized themselves into a body of earnest workers and carried on much philanthropic work. They established a night school for the Railway coolies. They also interested themselves in checking the abuses of the Assam coolie recruitment system. They successfully saved many a poor man and woman from a life of virtual slavery."[49] Haran Chandra Mitra, A Brahmo gentleman who was serving as a clerk at Hakanguri Tea Estate in upper Assam, started a night school for the benefit of the coolies.[50] He also tried to give religious instruction to them. *Brahmo Public Opinion* reports, "A Brahmo brother now serving as a clerk in one of the gardens of Assam, sends us the glad message that the Lord through his instrumentality has commenced a good work in the garden. A night school has been established for the benefit of the coolies, in which many of them assemble. Besides this religious instruction is given every Sunday. . . . Let us all help him with our prayers. . . ."[51]

Dwarka Nath and his followers wanted to project the problem of the plantation workers as a national issue and therefore tried their best to publicize the issue in all possible ways. Their efforts succeeded when the nationalist newspapers throughout the country endorsed their stand in respect to the Emigration Act the memorial they submitted to the Government of India. They succeeded in bringing a national consciousness about the fact that "the entire system of coolie labour in Assam was nothing but a form of slavery, the life of the Indian coolie being no better than that of the ancient slaves or the modern Negro-slaves."[52] But the Indian Association members also gradually realized that the government would not take any action against the European planters. *Sanjibani*, therefore, gave a call for self help. Appealing to the manhood of Indians, it suggested that "they should kindle such a fire in the land as will burn the Coolie Act into ashes."[53] Bipan Chandra comments, "Interestingly, though not surprisingly, no one in India at that time suggested self-help by the tea garden labourers themselves."[54] It is of equal interest to note that in the following years (which also followed Dwarka Nath Ganguli and Sivanath Sastri's visit to Assam in 1886) the tea garden workers started fighting back at the individual garden level in forms varying from absconding and occasional litigation to strikes and violent mass attack on the planters.[55] In 1899, Henry Cotton reported, "there is a growing tendency in the Coolie class to resent a blow by striking a blow in return and this soon leads to serious results, as the Coolies act in combination among themselves, and armed with formidable weapons—the implements of their industry; but this very tendency exercises a healthy influence in restraining the hot-headed and impetuous European assistant from raising his hand against them."[56]

In 1887 the Brahmo activists of the Indian Association tried their best to move a resolution to condemn "the legalized inhumanities of the Assam Cooly Act" and other issues related to the coolie problem at the Madras session of the Indian National Congress. But the Congress leadership stalled this move on the plea that it was a provincial, and not a national issue. Bepin Chandra Pal who was vocal about the "scandalous treatment meted out to the labourers in Assam" later lamented that the request was turned down by the Congress men on the ingenious ground that the matter, being a provincial subject, could not be discussed at the All-India Congress meeting.[57] But there the Congress leadership went wrong: statistics gives an altogether different picture as the labour force in Assam was drawn from the whole country. Out of the total tea garden labour force of the province of Assam in 1882, only 5.5 per cent were the indigenous population of Assam while 44.7 per cent belonged to Santhal Parganas, 27.2 per cent to Bengal, 21.6 per cent to North Western Provinces and 5 per cent came from the Southern part of India.[58] So, to term the coolie issue as a provincial matter did not have a valid reason. The members of the Indian Association had reasons to be frustrated at their failure move to this burning issue in the national political agenda during the annual session of the Indian National Congress in 1887.

Though the early efforts of tabling a resolution in the sessions of Indian National Congress failed, the Bengal political leaders organized the Bengal Provincial Conference which met annually since 1888. It needs to be mentioned that this provincial Conference was organized "primarily to express their strong views on the Assam coolie question. The Provincial Conference proved very successful and was transformed by the organizers into an annual affair. It always took keen and active interest in the problem of Assam coolies."[59] To highlight and discuss grievances related to regional problems, the Bengal Provincial Conference always took sympathetic resolutions supporting the cause of plantation workers of Assam. Needless to emphasize that Dwarka Nath and his followers were instrumental in its formation and they played an important role in its activities.

In the very first session of the Bengal Provincial Conference held in 1888 Dwarka Nath delivered a long speech highlighting the problems of the plantation workers of Assam. Dwarka Nath reported that he had actually seen dungeons where the runway coolies were illegally confined. In this Conference a resolution was adopted urging the government to appoint a Commission of Enquiry to look into the grievances of the coolies settled in the tea gardens of Assam. The Conference was presided by Mahendralal Sarkar. Appreciating the efforts of Dwarka Nath and his followers Sarkar said, "In passing this resolution you have given unmistakable indication of the sympathy, humanity which should be the guiding principle of all men, both as individuals and as forming the philanthropy community."[60] Proceedings of the Provincial Conference were widely publicized and the public sympathy went to such an extent that the *Bengalee* reported that the benefits that has arisen from the development of hidden resources (discovery of tea) "should not be secured by sacrificing the lives and liberties of a large section of Her Majesty's poorest, most ignorant and helpless subjects."[61]

There were other sections who were much more vocal on the issue who felt that economic and industrial development of India on the Planter-Raj line was totally undesirable and the new channel of squeezing the resources of India must be stopped. Two extracts from reports of *Sanjibani* reflects the belligerent mood of the Bengal intelligentsia on the issue. On 3 December 1987 it wrote that "the educated Indians should stop drinking of tea because drinking Assam tea is nothing more or less than drinking the blood of the poor persecuted coolie."[62] In another issue the newspaper advocated that "the tea trade should be ruined and Assam should become the abode of wild beasts than this fearful custom of selling coolies as slaves should be kept up."[63] The Sadharan Brahmo Samaj members brought out a special pamphlet coinciding the Provincial Conference which was distributed free among the delegates. The pamphlet contained several articles on problems of Assam tea garden coolies and the need of repealing the Act of 1889.

There are strong reasons to believe that it was due to the collective pressure of the Bengal Provincial Conference, the Indian Association and the Brahmo social reformists that the Act of 1882 was later partially revised by the Government. Because of their constant agitation a Commission of Enquiry to look into the grievances of the plantation labour was appointed in 1890. They were also instrumental in creating a pressure lobby among the nationalists of India. It was also due to the constant pressure put upon by this group of dedicated Brahmos that later in 1896 the coolie problem was included in the Congress agenda during its twelfth session of Indian National Congress held at Calcutta.[64] In this Congress detailed discussions were held on the Assam tea garden coolie issue. A resolution to repeal the Emigration Act was moved by Jogendra Chandra Ghosh. Bepin Chandra Pal seconded the proposal. Giving a graphic description of the tea garden coolie's fate, Ghosh said, "I have seen poor men and women jump overboard into the deep waters of the Brahmaputra to escape a lot which is worse than death. Bepin Chandra Pal seconded the proposal.

Supporting the resolution R.K. Sarkar said that "more barbarous provisions it will not be possible to find in any Act of the country."[65] The resolution was adopted by the Congress.

The Indian National Congress could no more ignore the burning issue for which the members of the Brahmo Samaj and the Indian Association were fighting for decades. The demand for repealing the Emigration Act was reiterated in the subsequent four sessions of the Congress. Government also could not ignore the issue any more and under nationalist pressure, it moved the Assam Labour and Emigration Bill in the Legislative Council on 13 March, 1899 thus fulfilling a demand of the members of the Brahmo Samaj and the Indian Association.

Notes and References

1. *Report on the Land Revenue Administration of the Lower Province, 1870-71 Govt. of Bengal*, Calcutta, 1872, p. 43-44
2. S.K. Bose, *Capital and Labour in Indian Tea Industry*, Bombay, 1954, p. 77. Bose writes that during the same period 55.6 per cent of the total coolies died at the Cheragaon Tea Estate of Cachar.
3. Amalendu Guha, *Planter Raj to Swaraj Freedom Struggle and Electoral Politics in Assam 1826-1947.* New Delhi, 1977, p. 18.
4. Sukomal Sen, *Working Class of India, History of the emergence and Movement,* Calcutta, 1977, p. 61.
5. Report of the Commissioner of Upper Assam on Tea Estates, *British Parliamentary Papers*, 1867, Paper 124, pp. 6-7.
6. Sir Bampfylde Fuller, *Some Personal Experiences*, London, 1930, pp. 117-19.
7. Sir Henry Cotton, *Indian and Home Memories*, London 1911.
8. *Ibid.*, p. 265.
9. H.K. Barpujari (ed.), *The Comprehensive History of Assam,* Vol. V, Guwahati, 1993, p. 50.
10. Dipankar Banerjee, Labour unrest in Assam: Some Aspects of the Labour Movement among the Non-plantation Workers [1919-39]. Unpublished M.Phil. dissertation, 1984. Submitted at Jawaharlal Nehru University, New Delhi, pp. 5-10.
11. Surendranath Banerjee's memorandum on behalf of the Indian Association to the Government of India, April, 1988 cited in Dipankar Banerjee, *ibid.*, p. 5.

12. Bipan Chandra, *Rise and Growth of Economic Nationalism in India,* New Delhi, 1966, Reprint 1991, p. 362.
13. *Dacca Prakash* was one of the first among the native newspapers in India which took up the cause of the tea planters in right earnest in 1862. The reporter of *Dacca Prakash* was compelled to give up his reports on tea garden coolies at a certain time as he was threatened by the planters.
14. *Somprakash*, Changripota, 1 and 9 June, 1862.
15. Tea garden labourers of Assam were generally referred to as "Coolies" in official and non-official records, including the contemporary newspapers and government records and the word found a place in the Oxford dictionary in 1890s.
16. David Kopf, *The Brahmo Samaj and the Shaping of the Modern Indian Mind*, Princeton, 1979, pp. 124-5.
17. Dipankar Banerjee, Centenary of the publication of *'Coolie Kahini'*: the role of Brahmo Samaj for the emancipation of plantation workers in Assam in retrospect, *Perspective*, Guwahati, 1988, pp. 6-16; also Prasenjit Chowdhury, Ramkumar Vidyaratna o tar Coolie Kahini, *Eka Ebong Koyekjon*, Guwahati, Autumn issue, Eighth year, 1987.

    Ramkumar's writings also portrayed the contemporary social condition of Assam as well. He wrote in *Coolie Kahini:* "Hospitals of this province are mostly full of *coolie* patients. Most of the local people do not go to the hospitals for the fear of being ostracised. The reasons being: (a) use of foreign medicines are injurious as caste sanctity of the individuals would be lost if such medicines are consumed; (b) patients from different caste and class take food together in the hospitals; (c) European doctors could not be trusted. (Ref.: Ramkumar Vidyaratna, *Coolie Kahini*, Calcutta, 1982 edn., p. 124.)
18. Biswanath Mukhopadhaya in his introduction in the third pre-centenary edition of Ramkumar Vidyaratna's *Coolie Kahini*, Calcutta, 1985, p. 14. Coolie Kahini was first published in 1888. A pre-centenary edition was published at the initiative of Gauranga Prasad Ghosh in 1982. A third edition of the book was published in 1885.
19. Sivanath Sastri, *op. cit.* and *Ramtanu Lahiri o Tatkalin Bango Samaj*, First published Calcutta, 1903, 1957 edition, p. 305.
20. Sivanath Sastri, *Atmacharita,* p. 247
21. Gautam Chattopadhaya, *Communism and Bengal's Freedom Movement*, Vol. 1, New Delhi, 1970, pp. 3-4.
22. Bipin Chandra Pal, *Memories of My Life and Times,* Vol. 1, Calcutta 1932, p. 246.
23. Dwarkanath Ganguly, *Slavery in British Dominion,* compiled by Kanai Lal Chattopadhaya, Calcutta, 1972.
24. Extract from Gohain Baruah's writing cited in Chowdhury, *op. cit.*, p. 157.
25. Chowdhury, *op. cit.*, pp. 80-81. *Translation ours*. Prasenjit Chowdhdhry has depicted in details this interesting debate between Balinarayan Bora and Lakhsmi Nath Bezbarua in his study.

26. Nagen Saikia ed., *Assam Bandhu*, Guwahati, 1984, p. 160. *Translation ours*.
27. Sukumar Sen, *Bangla Sahityer Itihas*, Calcutta, 1377 Bengali year, pp. 321, 516.
28. Pradyut Sengupta, *Banglar Sramik Jiban o Natya Sahitya*, Calcutta 1976.
29. Chowdhury, *op. cit.*, p. 109. *(*translation ours*).
30. Prabhat Chandra Ganguly, *Bharater Rastria Itihasher Khasra*, Calcutta, 1960, p. 87.
31. Bepin Chandra Pal, *Beginnings of the Freedom Movement in India*, Calcutta, 1959, p. 26.
32. *Ibid.*
33. Amalendu Guha, *op. cit.*, p. 41.
34. *Report of the Indian Association, 1892-1896*, Calcutta, pp. 22-27, 82-88.
35. *Twelfth Annual Report of the Indian Association*, Calcutta, 1887.
36. *Brahmo Public Opinion*, Calcutta, 18 Sept. 1988.
37. *Race and Ryots* was an English newspaper published from Calcutta during 1882 and 1894.
38. Prabhat Chandra Ganguly, *op. cit.*
39. Biswanath Mukherjee, *op. cit.*
40. Prabhat Chandra Ganguly, *op. cit.* The Brahmos also tried to handle the matter judiciously in tune with the prevailing nationalist sentiment, when they termed the murdered coolie girl as "daughter of India".
41. Gautam Chattopadhaya, *Communism and Bengal's Freedom Movement*, Vol. 1, New Delhi, 1970, pp. 3-4.
42. Amar Dutta, *Asame Chah Coolie Andolon o Dwarakanath*, Calcutta, 1978, p. 35-6.
43. Ajit Kumar Chakravarty, *Maharshi Devendra Nath Thakur*, Calcutta, 1971, p. 65.
44. *Mahapran Atul Chandra Roy: Sraddhanjali*, Small booklet, Calcutta, 1940. Nilmani Chakrabarty, Brahmo Missionary to Khasi Hills, has also mentioned in his autobiography about the help he received from Dr. Atul Chandra Roy when he first arrived at Dhubri on his way to Shillong.
45. *The Indian Messenger*, 14 Sept., 1884.
46. *The Indian Spectator*, Bombay, 15 January, 1882.
47. Bipan Chandra, *op. cit.*, pp. 367-9.
48. David Kopf, *The Brahmo Samaj and Shaping of the Modern Indian Mind*, Princeton, 1979, p. 144.
49. Sivanath Sastri, *History of the Brahma Samaj*, Calcutta 1911. Reprint 1993, p. 317.
50. *Brahmo Public Opinion*, Calcutta, 8 July, 1880.
51. *Ibid.*, 26 Feb. 1880.
52. Bipan Chandra, *op. cit.*, p. 369.
53. *Sanjivani*, 14 August, 1886.
54. Bipan Chandra, *op. cit.*, p. 372.

55. Amalendu Guha, *op. cit.*, p. 46.
56. P. Griffiths, *The History of the Tea Industry*, London, 1967, p. 32. (Henry Cotton's Report cited by Griffiths.)
57. Bepin Chandra Pal, *Memories of My Life and Times*, Calcutta, 1932, Vol. II, pp. 54-55.
58. Prabhat Chandra Ganguly, *op. cit.*; also Dipankar Banerjee, *Perspective, op. cit.*, p. 12.
59. Bipan Chandra, *op. cit.*, p. 366.
60. Prabhat Chandra Ganguly, *op. cit.*
61. *Bengalee*, 11 March, 1993.
62. *Sanjibani*, 7 Dec., 1887.
63. *Ibid.*, 19 Nov. 1887.
64. *Report of the Indian National Congress*, Twelfth Session (Calcutta session), 1986, p. 138.
65. *Ibid.*, pp. 165-70.

4

CONCLUSION

The Brahmo Samaj was, without doubt, an influential pioneer of the Hindu reform movement in the beginning of the nineteenth century. It played a significant role in the renaissance of not only Bengal, but also other parts of the country. In north-east India its ideals and principles might not have attracted as many followers as Samaj fraternity or missionaries would have wished, nonetheless it could with pride say that it was able to inspire enlightenment and modern thinking. The movement remained confined among the elite few, except perhaps in the Khasi hills, nevertheless Brahmoism made a definite contribution of rationalism, freedom of thought and growth of nationalism besides influencing far-reaching changes in the socio-cultural and intellectual life of the people of the region.

In the Brahmaputra valley it paved the way for social regeneration. Samaj members tried to rid the then society of its ills and inequalities by battling for equal educational opportunities for girls, elimination of child marriage and polygamy and removal of stigma on widowhood. Schools were opened at the Samaj's initiative and Brahmos contributed to the development of Assamese literature and journalism. In the Khasi hills Brahmo ideals and missionary activities were able to set in motion a rural reconstruction movement, while walking hand in hand with Unitarians and supplementing the efforts of Christian missionaries to initiate modern thinking among the peoples. But, all said and done, perhaps the movement's momentous contribution in the region will always remain its intense efforts to mobilize public opinion in favour of the oppressed plantation workers in the tea gardens of Assam. It is due in most part to Brahmo missionaries Ramkumar Vidyaratna and Dwarka Nath Ganguly's writings that the attention of the educated intelligentsia and political circle was drawn to the distressing plight of the *coolies,* and the Assam Labour and Emigration Bill finally passed to alleviate their condition.

Believing that example is better than precept, most Brahmo Samaj members set example through their own lives, and played pioneering roles in many aspects. Gunabhiram Baruah who did his utmost to spread the message of the Brahmo faith by writing articles on women's education, polygamy, child marriage and widow remarriage himself married a widow. Padmahash Goswami augmented Baruah's hard work. In spite of a hostile society he remained steady in his belief, thereby motivating some youths to convert to theism.

Nilmani Chakravarty broke new ground by opening missions in different places in Khasi hills and selflessly serving the people. He encouraged freedom of thought by aiding Hajom Kissor Singh begin the Unitarian movement in the hills. Jeeban Roy, the apostle of Khasi renaissance and the man who founded the *Seng Khasi,* a sociocultural organization for the promotion of the indigenous Khasi religion based on the belief of God as creator with due respect for ancestors, was also influenced throughout his life by Brahmo ideals. The Samaj's role in the emancipation of Khasi society too cannot be underrated. Schools, libraries and sociocultural activity became the leitmotif of the Samaj's action in Shillong and other places in the hills. Its progressive ideas struck a chord in the minds of the egalitarian tribal peoples and Brahmo aficionados swelled in numbers.

When the Brahmo ideas entered Assam towards the second half of the nineteenth century, the society of Assam was too conservative and a closed one to be influenced by new reform movements that was sweeping over some other parts of India, particularly Bengal. The entire north-east India and for that effect Assam came under British rule quite late compared to Bengal. Naturally liberal ideas of the West could not make an early infiltration here. Though the process of social transformation and overall development here was delayed , it could not be prevented. And it is in this context the role of Brahmo movement need to be examined—the Brahmo Samaj despite of its small number of followers in Assam acted as a catalyst of transformation.

Education brings enlightenment. The Brahmos took at the task of promoting educational activities in different places of undivided Assam in right earnest. But they did it in true philanthropic zeal, not with the ulterior objective of proselytization. They made genuine contribution to spread knowledge with a dedication and selfless spirit. Sumanta Neyogi in his book *The Brahmo Samaj and Development of Education* (Delhi, 1986) observed: "The educational activities of the Brahmos clearly bring out a moving fact that the Brahmos took spread of education as an essential part of their religious activity. There were three categories of Brahmos engaged in the promotion of education. The first group comprised of missionaries who fully devoted themselves to educational activities. The second group consisted of Brahmos who had been employed somewhere but devoted themselves to the work of education, either leaving the job or continuing with it. The third category of Brahmos consisted of individuals who were neither missionaries nor employed somewhere, but fully absorbed with the educational activities of the Samaj. Of course, individuals belonging to all the categories were intimately attached to the cause of education." This observation is true in case of Assam also. We have noticed involvement of all these three categories of Brahmos in the spread of education in Assam in the present study. Their important contribution of the Samaj towards spreading of primary and secondary education in places like Dhubri, Shillong, Nagaon, Silchar, Tezpur and Khasi hills remains unquestionable. Schools were opened both for the boys and the girls.

They also promoted literacy and cultural activities in the

region. The Samaj also helped in the emotional integration of different communities and thus acted a cementing force. Assam's great litterateur Ambikagiri Roy Chowdhury mentioned in his writings how many community functions and official programmes in schools in Assam during the beginning of the twentieth century always started with a *Brahmo Sangeet* or Brahmo prayer song.

The Brahmo Samaj provided an intellectual forum in the towns where it was set up. Along with the Brahmos, many non-Brahmo social activists, scholars, pundits, journalists and many individuals interested in gaining something from the world of knowledge found a common and convenient forum in the Brahmo Samaj. Another important aspect of Brahmo Samajists' commitment towards promotion of knowledge could be noticed in its effort to establish libraries in different places of Assam. Where ever a Brahmo Samaj prayer hall was established, schools and libraries were established there inevitably. We have seen that some earliest libraries at places like Silchar, Shillong, Guwahati, Dhubri and Tezpur were established by the Brahmos.

The Brahmo Samaj encouraged inter-caste or inter-community marriages, thereby paving the way for a democratic social structure and intermingling among communities. By introducing Sankardev's *borgeets* in Brahmo prayers both Goswami and Baruah did immense service in bringing Assamese people closer to the Brahmo faith. Moreover, the literary efforts made by many Brahmos in Assam went a long way in stimulating new thoughts and contributing to the treasure of Assamese literature and journalism. Journals, newspapers and booklets like *Assam Mihir, Assam Darpan, Chandrodoi, Assam Bandhav, Digvijay Gyanodoi, Brahmo Dharmar Lakkhan, Brahmo Dharma Kakno Bole, Assam Hitoishi Patrika, Koh Pantha* and *Assam Bandhu* were all effected by Brahmo sensibilities.

Brahmo missionary Nilmani Chakravarty took lead in setting up schools and dispensaries in remote areas in the Khasi hills and fighting for causes and issues on the people's behalf, thereby giving them hope for a better life. In his zeal for enlightening the people and showing them a better way of life Nilmani taught villagers modern methods of agriculture and horticulture and created a consciousness against intoxicating liquor and drugs. He wrote poems, hymns, articles, essays and prayer books in Khasi and contributed his mite to the development of Khasi literature. And although Nilmani's contribution in the Khasi hills was above par, there were many other committed Brahmos who supplemented his efforts to spread the faith's message in many other ways.

Albeit Brahmo Samaj missionaries also did make fervent efforts to expose the sorry plight of the tea plantation workers of Assam, but how far they were able to shape the minds of the workers is yet a matter of debate. Most times Ramkumar Vidyaratna and Dwarka Nath Ganguly had to understand the lives in tea gardens surreptitiously and under cover. Rarely, if ever, was either of the two missionaries able to address the workers about the teachings of Brahmoism. Products of a new spirit of enquiry the Brahmos were stung by the untold misery and virtual serfdom of the *coolies* and made all-out efforts to throw light on an issue that was often swept under the carpet by the Planter Raj. And these efforts appear to be totally altruistic, bereft of any aggressive motive of converting workers to theism.

Tea estate lives were discussed in Samaj meetings in the general framework of its social reform programme. Vidyaratna's personal account of exploitation in the tea gardens in articles published in Brahmo newspapers played a historic role in drawing the attention of nationalists. Dwarka Nath Ganguly's articles had a similar impact and in no small measure awakened the latent nationalism of the people. And, with the Brahmo Samaj and the Indian Association, the two most important forums of the late nineteenth century India, carrying on a continuous campaign on the *coolie* problem, other nationalist forums too picked up the issue; in the twelfth session of the Congress in 1896 the tea garden *coolie* problem was discussed in detail. In four subsequent sessions thereafter demand was raised for repealing the Emigration Act.

In conclusion it must be said that the Brahmo Samaj was able to leave behind a lasting impression in the region's socio-cultural life. Agreed that many a time its role in paving changes is not visible or appreciated; but history would beg to differ. The Samaj undoubtedly played a catalytic role in overlaying the path for a renaissance of sorts in the north-east, somewhat like the one that had already begun in Bengal then.

APPENDIX A

REPORT ON BRAHMO SAMAJ ACTIVITIES IN THE KHASI HILLS

> "In April the Shillong Brahmo Samaj received a letter from some Khasi gentlemen of Shella in which they expressed a wish to be informed of the principles of Brahmoism. This letter was forwarded to the Executive Committee of the Sadharan Brahmo Samaj. In view of the desire of the Khasis themselves to know what Brahmoism is, the Executive Committee felt that it was incumbent upon them to take steps for the establishment of a Brahmo mission in the Khasi Hills. At first there was some difficulty in finding a worker. But it was soon overcome, as Babu Nilmani Chakravarti, a candidate for ordination as a missionary of the Sadharan Brahmo Samaj, expressed his willingness to proceed to the Khasi Hills. The Executive Committee at once resolved to send him to Shillong to report upon the state of things there. Favourable reports having been received from him, our friend was requested to stay and work in the Khasi Hills; and sometime after the Committee proceeded to ordain him as one of their missionaries."

Thus commenced the Khasi Mission of the Samaj, which now forms an important part of its work. It has passed through many vicissitudes of fortune including the great earthquake of 1897, which caused heavy damage to the properties of the Mission. But the first missionary still sticks to his post and has succeeded in making the mission a source of moral and spiritual influence amongst the population of these hills. In course of time he transferred his mission centre from Shillong to Cherapoonji, where it is at present situated. The work has expanded in his hands. Shella and some other hill-stations have come in to be included in the Khasi Hills Mission, which is still being persistently carried on by Brother Nilmani Chakravarti with the help of a few workers. The people love and revere him. He is their patron-saint, their friend and guide. He has published tracts in the Khasi language which have helped a good deal in spreading the principles of the new faith amongst those people. When the Khasi Mission was started, Maharshi Devendranath received Nilmani Chakravarti with open arms, and as a mark of his sympathy placed in his hands a respectable sum as his donation and also went on regularly helping him.

The missionaries of the Samaj visited during the year 44 places in Bengal, 24 in Bihar, 3 in Chotanagpur, 12 in Assam, 4 in the N.W. Provinces and in the Western Presidency and as the result of their mission operations eight new Samajes were established, one Mandir was consecrated, the foundations of two others were laid, and ten ladies and thirty gentlemen were elected as new members of the Samaj during the year.

(Extract from the Annual Report of Brahmo Samaj for the year 1889 regarding its work in the Khasi Hills. The report also mentions that in 1889 Brahmo Missionaries visited 12 places in Assam.)

(*Source: History of the Brahmo Samaj* by Sivanath Sastri, Calcutta, 1911, pp. 318-20.)

APPENDIX B

REPORT ON THE KHASI MISSION
(Sivanath Sastri's Report of 1911)

Now I must proceed to briefly review the short but interesting history of the Khasi Mission of the Sadharan Brahmo Samaj with its headquarters at Cherrapunji on the Khasi Hills.

The mission was duly founded in 1889. Brother Nilmani at once made up his mind to live amongst them, to be one of them and to do everything in his power to educate and elevate them. He took his first abode at Shillong, the headquarters of the Hills; but within a short time transferred his sphere of work to Cherrapunji, where a regular mission centre has been built up in course of time. He commenced his work by taking to the earnest study of the Khasi language, over which he soon acquired mastery, and began to hold weekly services and conversational meetings with the people in their own language. As a part of his regular work, be opened something like a charitable homoeopathic dispensary, where he daily distributed medicine to poor people. Within a short time the hill people began to look upon him as their true friend and benefactor and men and women began to flock to the services of the Samaj. The movement has gone on ever since, till the number of Brahmos who have joined the communion has risen to nearly 500. Samajes have come to be established amongst the hill people in other stations than Cherrapunji. The number of these branch Samajes has come up to 12 up to this time [1911] and Brahmoism may be fairly said to have taken root amongst these people.

Almost all these branch Samajes have a variety of institutions attached to them for propagatory and other work, all carried on by the Khasis themselves, a great proof of the success of the Mission. A list of these branch Samajes is given below.

1. Mawblei Brahmo Samaj (Cherrapunji): This is the

headquarters of the Mission. Institutions attached to it: (1) Women's Samaj, (2) Children's Samaj, (3) The Sangat, (4) The Children's School, (5) The Weekly Conversational Meeting, (6) The Homoeopathic Dispensary, (7) The weekly family prayer meetings, (8) A weekly prayer meeting in a neighbouring village called Mawkisiem. (Has got a mission house.)

2. Nongrim Brahmo Samaj. Institution: a school. (No Mandir.)
3. Nongthymmai Brahmo Samaj (Mawsmai). Institution: a school. (Has got a Mandir.)
4. Mawlong Brahmo Samaj. Institution: the Sangat and a weekly night meeting. (Has got a Mandir.)
5. Sasarat Brahmo Samaj. (No Mandir.)
6. Nongwar Brahmo Samaj. (No Mandir.)
7. Laitkynsew Brahmo Samaj. Institution: a dispensary. (Has got a small mission house, but no Mandir.)
8. Mawstoh Brahmo Samaj. Institutions. (1) Sangat, (2) Women's meeting, (3) Weekly conversational meetings. (Has got a Mandir.)
9. Sohlap Brahmo Samaj. Institutions: Sangat, women's meeting, weekly conversational meetings. (Has got a Mandir.)
10. Disong Brahmo Samaj (Shella). (Has got a Mandir.)
11. Wahlong Brahmo Samaj. Institutions: Sangat and weekly family prayer meeting. (Has got a small house for meetings.)
12. Mawkhar Brahmo Samaj (Shillong). Institutions: Dispensary, a Bengali class. (Has got a Mandir.)

Nor is Brother Nilmani single-handed in his work at present. Five young men have come forward to offer themselves for service under him. The first of them is Sriman Umesh Chandra Chaudhuri. He is a native of Sylhet. Umesh Chandra is an old worker. He was for some time connected with the Rammohun Roy Seminary of Bankipur as a teacher, whence he has transferred his services to the Khasi Hills. The second is Sriman

Surjamani Roy, a Khasi by birth, who is in charge of four neighbouring Samajes, with Laitkynsew as his headquarters, The third and the fourth are Srimans Rohinikanta Roy and Ashwathama Roy, working under Nilmani Chakravarti at Cherrapunji. The fifth is Sriman Bangsabhushan Roy, who has graduated from Dr. M.M. Bose's Homoeopathic School and is stationed at Mawkhar in Shillong.

With the help of these the work of the Khasi Mission is going on with vigour at present. Brahmoism has taken hold of these hill tribes and has organised itself as a distinct influence.

It is also a noteworthy fact that the Khasi Mission has been indirectly useful towards the modification of the educational system on the Khasi Hills. The representations of our missionary were accepted and several changes have been introduced into that system. His exertions have also been incessant towards checking the course of intemperance amongst the hill people, from which they are horribly suffering.

(*Source: History of the Brahmo Samaj* by Sivanath Sastri, Calcutta, 1911, pp. 437-39.)

APPENDIX C

REPORT ON PANDIT RAMKUMAR VIDYARATNA'S VISIT AT DIFFERENT PLACES OF ASSAM (AS REPORTED IN NEWSPAPERS)

(i) On the 31st Ultimo Baboo Ram Coomar Bhuttacharjea delivered another lecture in the English School (Nagaon). The subject was "Hope of Prospects of India". There were about 250 persons present on this occasion and all were pleased with the speech. It was very impressive and eloquent and full of instructive matter. He compared India with a human body and said that, as the different members of the body complete the whole body. So the different countries of India make the whole India. And as one part of the body sympathises with the pleasures and pains of the other parts, so all the countries of India ought to sympathise with one another. He dwelt on the future prospects of India and said that social, moral, religious, and intellectual reformations are necessary. He added that the religion preached by the Brahmo Samaj is the only religion that can regenerate India.

The audience left the hall with useful and interesting matters to think on.

We want such missionaries to stir the mind of the people.

May the labours of this beloved missionary we have among us prove fruitful.

*　　*　　*

(ii) Pandit Ram Kumar Bhattacharjea visited Biswanath on the 31st Srabun last. On the 6th Bhadra he came to Shibsagore and remained there more than a week spending his time in conducting Divine service, holding religious conversation and delivering lectures. The two public speeches he gave there were on "Ancient Bards of India" and "Religious Revolution created by Sankar and Chaitanya". He is on his way to Tezpore.

The name of the Brahmin of Nowgoing who lately threw

up his holy thread is Baboo Anunda Ram Goswami. We learn he has been overwhelmed with persecutions but we hope faith in God will keep him harmless.

(*Source: Brahmo Public Opinion*, 12 September, 1878.)

* * *

(iii) The following letter gives an account of the doings of Baboo Ram Coomar Bhuttacharjea arrived here on the 21st instant and delivered a lecture in the English School house on the 24th August on Ancient poet; he dwelt mainly on the two creations of God, the matter and human soul. The attendance was rather scanty on account of incessant rains. A prayer meeting was held the next day in the house of Babu Jagat Chundra Das, B.L. After the service, it was determined to begin again the Somaj and until the house is rebuilt the service will take place in the above mentioned house.

(*Source: Brahmo Public Opinion*, 15 August, 1878.)

* * *

(iv) A correspondent sends us the following account of Pandit Ram Kumar Bhuttacharjya's visit to Tezpore.

The Pandit arrived here on Saturday the 17th Instant and conducted divine service of the Central Assam Upasana Somaj in the evening.

On Sunday he visited several leading Assamese gentlemen in their houses and conversed with them on religious and social topics. No public meeting of any kind was held in the evening lest it should interfere with the evening service of the "Tezpur Brahmo Samaj".

On Monday evening he read and expounded certain parts of the Upanishad to an audience consisting of Brahmos and non-Brahmos, Assamese and Bengalis.

A series of three sermons were preached on Wednesday, Thursday and Friday evenings.

At the special request of a non-Brahmo gentleman the Pandit delivered a public lecture on Saturday afternoon, on "Inspiration and Mediator". There was an unexpectedly large gathering on the occasion. In the evening he conducted divine service in the

Central Assam Upasana Somaj. The lecture was very interesting to the understanding portion of the audience who had read the history of the late schism in the Brahmo Somaj.

Besides these there were prayer meetings held in the houses of several of the local Brahmos; they were attended by the Brahmos and Brahmicas of the place except a very few adherents of Babu K.C. Sen.

The Pandit proceeds to Debrugurh by the next upward steamer.

(*Source: Brahmo Public Opinion*, 6 May, 1886.)

* * *

(v) A friend writes from Shillong—

> Pandit R.K. Vidyaratna arrived here at the latter part of July and worked in our midst for more than three weeks. As he was invited by the Inspector of Schools to attend the educational conference as a non-official member, much of his time was spent in the conference affairs.

In the mornings he visited the residents of the station and the evening conducted service of the prayer meetings held at the house of the Brahmos and others.

The last day of July was a day of great rejoicing for the Shillong Brahmos; it was the day on which the new Prayer Hall of the Shillong Brahmo Samaj was consecrated. In the morning there was a Sankirtan procession from the house of the Secretary to the New Mandir. In spite of unfavourable weather, there was a large gathering consisting of people of different sects and the name of the Lord was sung very enthusiastically. After the procession was over there was Divine Service in the Mandir conducted by Pandit Vidyaratna. The Service was very impressive. The afternoon was spent in reading and individual prayers. In the evening there was the usual service.

Some of our friends from the plains, who had been invited to attend the conference, very heartily joined us and contributed not a little to the success of the consecration ceremony.

(*Source: The Indian Messenger*, 4 September 1887.)

APPENDIX D

CONDOLENCE RESOLUTION OF THE SADHARAN BRAHMO SAMAJ, CALCUTTA ON THE DEMISE OF PADMAHASH GOSWAMI

(i) The Brahmo Somaj

With deep regret we hope to announce the untimely death of Pandit Padmahash Goswami of Assam. He was attacked with small-pox and died on the 19th of Bysakh last. From the establishment of the Sadharan Brahmo Samaj, he was one of our most valuable workers as a lay-missionary. Though engaged as a teacher in the education department, he would devote all the time he could spare to the preaching and propagation of our faith. He was single handed and alone when he first embraced theism, but by his noble zeal and perseverance soon succeeded in getting around him a band of sympathisers and friends. Many through his influence accepted the principles of Brahmanism and some of them have joined the Samaj in the face of terrible social persecutions. We recommended to our readers the short account of his mission work, in our last Annual Report for study. In him the Sadharan Brahmo Somaj has lost a valuable co-adjutor and the province of Assam a zealous disinterested sincere and kind hearted religious reformer who was the centre of a new life.

(*Source: Brahmo Public Opinion*, 15 May, 1879.)

*   *   *

(ii) Sir,—It is with the deepest regret that I have to record the death of Babu Padmahash Goswami, a young Assamese reformer of great parts. He was lately attacked by small-pox to which he succumbed on the 1st instant. A man full of energy and enthusiasm, distinguished alike for the love of his country and his religion, he was ever dear to his countrymen. He was looked forward to as a champion of a party of young men who would revolutionise society. And his death at a time, when social and religious activity in Assam had just begun, and when his assistance was so necessary, will be severely felt not only by the Assamese but by all persons interested in the cause of social and religious progress in India. In him Assam has lost one of her noblest sons and the Brahmo Samaj one of its most indefatigable workers.

Babu Padmahash Goswami was descended from one of the most distinguished Goswami families of Assam. When he was about 12 years of age, he was sent to a tol in Kamrup. For sometime he studied Sanskrit with diligence. From his early age, he was of a religious turn of mind, but he was very inquisitive. Instead of remaining satisfied with what his teacher taught him, the young Goswami used to ask them questions which they were at their wits' end to answer. As he grew in years, his faith in the Shastras begun to wane less and less. The spirit of his enquiry having produced an alteration between himself and his gurus, he went to Gauhati, where, for sometime, he prosecuted his studies. His attention was directed towards Brahmoism, and in 1870, when a Samaj was established at Gauhati, he at once found in it an object of his sympathy. From this time he became a Brahmo. Shortly after, he went to his native place, Nowgong. Here he publicly burnt is sacred paita in the presence of his guru, his parents, and his kinsmen. And though for this piece of sacrilege, he was obliged to leave home, he was afterwards received back in the bosom of the family. From the time that he was driven out of home up to his death he worked incessantly for the welfare of his country. He diffused among his countrymen scientific, moral and religious truths by means of lectures, tracts, periodicals &c. He was a regular contributor to some of the distinguished magazines of Bengal and to most of the newspapers in Assam. He was the Editor of the *Assam Darpan* and the *Inanodoy*, a scientific journal in Assamese. During all this time he was struggling violently against the corruptions in the Hindu society and the Hindu religion on the one hand, and refuting the attacks of the Christian missionaries on the other. Besides, he was the Secretary to the Nowgong Brahmo Samaj, and it was mainly to his exertions that its flourishing condition was due. And such was his influence that even the Goswamis of Aooniati, the very centre of Brahmonical superstitions in Assam, could not but look upon him with peculiar awe and reverence. In the late scism of the Brahmo Samaj a radical and a conscientious man like Padmahash could not be expected to side with Keshub Babu's party, and it is too well-known to need mentioning here that he joined the Sadharan Brahmo Samaj. Padmahash was about 27 years of age. He was frank and amiable though resolute and full of fire. He silently won the love of his countrymen by his patriotic zeal, his honesty of purpose, and the singular purity of his character. And though he himself has passed away and the dust has returned to dust, his spirit shall survive him as long as Truth will endure.

Yours Sincerely
Abhay Sankar Guha

Calcutta
The 12th May, 1879

(*Source: Brahmo Public Opinion*, 22 May, 1879.)

*   *   *

(iii) The annual report of this year notices with sorrow the death of Brother Padmahash Goswami, a young Assamese, who had been drawn into the Brahmo Samaj some years before and had joined the Sadharan Brahmo Samaj as a member of its Committee. He was working single handed in Assam, propagating the new principles and had been put to much persecution on that account. He died during this year, when he was below thirty, deeply mourned by all who knew him. He left behind him a precious legacy of an inspiring memory in some newly awakened souls.

*   *   *

(iv) The Executive Committee of the Sadharan Brahmo Samaj have passed the following resolution on the much lamented death of Babu Padmahash Goswami of Nowgoing, Assam:

"That the Committee records its deepest grief and sorrow at the news of the untimely death of their revered and beloved friend and co-adjuter, Babu Padmahash Goswami, an unflinching advocate and earnest preacher of the truths of Brahmoism in the province of Assam, who by his life and work has left a glorious example for others to follow".

"And that Pandit Ram Kumar Bhattacharya be requested to write a sketch of his life by an early date with a view to be published either in the Tatva-Kawmudi or in a separate pamphlet".

(*Source: Brahmo Public Opinion*, 29 May, 1879.)

APPENDIX E

INTERESTING REPORTS/LETTERS ON DIFFERENT ISSUES RELATED TO ASSAM IN BRAHMO NEWSPAPERS

(i) *Report on Sibsagar*

Sir,—Sibsagar is a place situated near the extremity of Assam. It is surrounded by mountains. The climate is healthy and delightful. But it is growing hotter day by day. Formerly Cholera was unknown here. Now it appears yearly and of late, monthly. Another new disease has taken root. It is called leg-swelling. The very name will indicate what sort of disease it is. The Civil Medical Officer ascribes it to the Bazar oil.

A cyclone, we read in "Oroonaday" took place at Nazira. The place lies close to Sibsagar. Several roofs were blown off and houses levelled to the ground. But happily no life has been lost.

The monsoon sky-races here ended yesterday. The race ground was crowded to suffocation.

The Zila School here, will, I hear, be henceforth called the Sibsagar High English School. But it is merely a change of name.

A friend from Nowgong wrote that some scholarships and free studentships will be awarded to preserve the memory of the late Mr. P. Goswamy of Nowgong. The Brahmo Samaj will publish an account of his life.

Yours sincerely
TRUTH

Sibsagar
The 15th June, 1879

(*Source: The Indian Messenger*, 26 June, 1879.)

(ii) *Report on Goalpara Zamindars' Objection*

The Zemindars of Goalpara have addressed a memorial to

the Government of India on the subject of the Assam Local Rates Regulation. They complain first that the Regulation is unnecessary. In the second place, they very justly complain that whereas in Bengal, the Public Works Cess is levied for the purpose of famine relief only, in Assam they would be applied also to local purpose. In the next place, they complain, and we think with great justice, that whereas in Bengal, the Public Works Cess is levied upon the gross collections in Assam, an arbitrary rate of Rs.2 per acre has been fixed, and they show that the gross collections do not exceed 8 as per acre. We hope the Government of India will give careful consideration to the memorial, and meet the just demands of the Assam zemindars.

(*Source: Brahmo Public Opinion*, 3 June, 1880.)

*   *   *

(iii) *Report on Shifting Headquarters of Goalpara District to Dhubri*

With the approval of the Government of India, the Chief Commissioner is pleased to notify that headquarters of the district of Goalpara have been transferred from the station of Goalpara to the station of Dhubri, with effect from the 24th instant, on which date the district treasury was opened at Dhubri.

The Chief Commissioner is also pleased to notify that the former sub-division of Dhubri, with the addition of Duars, Bijni and Sibli, will henceforth constitute the sudder sub-division of the Goalpara district.

The Chief Commissioner is further pleased to notify that the late sudder sub-division of Goalpara, excepting Duars, Sibli, and Bijni will henceforth constitute the sub-division of Goalpara.

(*Source: Brahmo Public Opinion*, 15 January, 1885.)

*   *   *

(iv) *Report on Jorehat Sub-Division*

The following telegram from Jorehat, Assam, appeared in the *Indian Mirror*—the inhabitants of the Jorehat Sub-Division are greatly aggrieved by and dissatisfied with the result of the working of the Local Board. The Native members find it impossible to do their duties towards their constituencies owing to the negligence and unwillingness of the District Engineer to carry out their projects. The District Engineer has practically reduced the Board to a mere subordinate body. It is hoped the leading members Messrs. Bezboruah and Borah will bring the whole state of affairs to the notice of the Government. Unless Government strengthens the authority of the Local Boards they will prove a mere show, specially when they will have to deal with European officers.

(*Source: The Indian Messenger*, 21 June, 1885.)

* * *

(v) *Report on Assam Conference at Tezpur*

Tezpore, December 6—The Assam Conference held its first sitting at the Tezpore Town Hall on the 5th December from 2 to 5 in the afternoon. The districts of Dibrugarh, Sibsagar, Nowgong and Tezpore were represented by sixteen delegates, beside a large number of representatives from the interior of the Tezpore district. The meeting was presided over by Baboo Haribilash Agorewallah of Tezpore. Baboo Radhanath Changkakati of Dibrugarh was elected Secretary for one year at this day's sitting. A routine of business was only promulgated and adopted. The first proposal was the election of delegates for the Indian National Congress, which was very warmly discussed and adjourned to the next day.—*Statesman*.

(*Source: The Indian Messenger*, 11 December, 1887.)

* * *

(vi) *Letter on the Problem of the Clerks in Assam Government Service*

Sir,—The Legislative machinery is always working or rather over working; we see a bill introduced to regulate labour in factories. Is legislation at all necessary when the labourers are quite content and they willingly employ themselves in the work and we generally see these persons in good health? On the other hand some such steps should have been taken for the well being of the wretched keranis. These under-paid persons are often required to labour more than six hours, sometimes ten or twelve, even the Government offices. Though there is a fixed time in all government offices it is rarely observed in the muffossil. Even in holidays &c the writers here are called to work under the penalty of forfeiting their appointments. These things are frequently to be observed in a Deputy Commissioner's office than anywhere else. Under these circumstances how difficult it is to serve with a salary barely sufficient to support a man with his family, having no leisure to ply for any other means. Not to say of trying other means very little time is allowed for relaxation. Some of the Hajurs are so very generous as to refuse to grant leave for a few weeks when it is asked after a dozen of years' continuous services. We humbly beseech, that our kind Government will take these into consideration and rescue the poor keranis from such inhumanity.

G.C.C.

Sibsagore

(*Source: Brahmo Public Opinion*, 27 March, 1879.)

* * *

(vii) *Letter on the Out-Still System in Cachar*

Sir,—I find from your last issue that the Cachar tea planters are crying out loudly against the ravages of the Outstill system among the coolies, and that the Chief Commissioner's remedy is to get the planters themselves to become Outstillers!

I would suggest an improvement or an amendment. Do away with the cheap and nasty out still liquor altogether and get good Saddar-distilled spirits to be sold to the coolies (who will have it) at a proper price of about one rupee per bottle, and let the sale be under the supervision of the planters, and if I am not greatly mistaken they will soon get rid of drunkenness from the tea gardens of Cachar.

The only real remedy for drunkenness among the poor in India is to raise the price of liquor as high as possible so as to be beyond the reach of temptation to the mass of the people, but as long as the Out-stills are in vogue this is impossible, therefore, the only alternative is to abolish the system both in the country and the towns and I feel pretty sure it must come to this if the Government is in right earnest in its intentive to prevent the spread of drunkenness in the land as we have good reason to believe from the action already taken by Sir Rivers Thompson who I have no doubt has the good of the people nearer at heart than the increase of revenue to the State. Petitions to this effect should be sent up to the Bengal Government.

THOMAS EVANS

Mussori

(*Source: The Indian Messenger*, 3 May, 1885.)

* * *

(viii) *Report on Number of Widow and Widowers in Assam*

There are in Assam 2,210 widows under fifteen, 115,229 between fifteen and forty, and 250,846 above forty years of age. The total number of widowers is only 84,666. Yet the number of males in the population everywhere largely exceeds the females.

(*Source: The Indian Messenger*, 15 June, 1884.)

APPENDIX F

HIGHER EDUCATION IN ASSAM: BRAHMO SAMAJ ADVOCACY FOR RE-ESTABLISHMENT OF COLLEGE CLASSES OF GOUHATI HIGH SCHOOL

The Assam Hitakari Sabha has submitted a memorial to the Chief Commissioner of Assam, for the re-establishment of College classes of the Gouhati High School which were abolished in 1876. We regret we cannot make room for the memorial which seems to us to be very well-drawn; and the facts and arguments used by our brethren in this memorial seem to us be almost unanswerable. It is indeed a pity that there should not be a College in the whole Assam, and that the students who are poor, should have to come to Bengal to complete their education. The effect has been this; out of 24 Assamese students who passed the Entrance since 1875, about one third could not prosecute their studies, although six of them had obtained scholarships. The memorial shows that while nine Assamese students passed the first Arts from the Gouhati High school during the eight years of its existence, not more than two passed the same Examination from other schools, since the abolition of the College classes. The memorial proves from reports of the Inspector of schools that the abolition of the Higher classes has materially affected the cause of high education in Assam, with regard to the cost of education the memorial shows that although at the time of abolishing the College classes, the cost was so high as Rs.774-4 per each student, still it was less than the cost in Berhampore College. Sanskrit College and Cuttack College in certain years and Cuttack College in shews that in that very year there were saving of Rs.26,000 and of Rs.18,683—portion of which might have been converted to Gouhati High School. There will be about 18 students. We cannot sufficiently commend the laudable efforts of the memorialists in the cause of high education, and we hope Sir Stuart Baylay will grant their prayer.

(*Source: Brahmo Public Opinion*, 1 July, 1880.)

APPENDIX G

REPORT ON NOWGUNG (NAGAON) BRAHMO SAMAJ IN THE *BRAHMO PUBLIC OPINION*

Proceedings of a meeting of the Nowgung (Assam) Brahmo Samaj held on the 17th August, 1879.

The Secretary explained the object of the meeting as below:

> I have two objects in convening this meeting—First—To keep the memory of our late lamented brother and Secretary Padmahash Goswami in connection with our Samaj, and secondly to secure an estate for the Samaj, yielding an income of about Rs.27. There is a piece of rent-paying land in this town. It is about 1¾ Bighas in area and situated at a distance of about 40 yards from the Mandir. The owner has fixed the price of the land at Rs.300, though it is probable that he might demand thirty per cent more as there are several competitors for the purchase of the land. I therefore propose that funds be collected by subscription to the extent of Rs.425, in order to purchase the land, from all friends, admirers and sympathisers of Padmahash, and the Brahmo Samaj. The estate when purchased will be called "Padmahash Estate". It is to be the property of the Nowgong (Assam) Brahmo Samaj. The above was carried unanimously.

1. *Resolved:* That the Secretary be directed to collect subscriptions in this town as well as from other places. That letters be written to the following gentleman asking them for aid:

   Mr. Phukan
   Mr. Baruah
   Babu Mohim Chandra Chakraverti

Babu Ram Durlav Mazoomdar
Babu Dina Nath Sen
Babu Lakhi Kanta Dass
Babu Uday Ram Das

2. The letters be also written to the following Somajes for the same purpose; Sadharan (Calcutta), Dacca, Cuttack, Julpiguree, Dhubri, Sibsagor and Goalpara Brahmo Samajes.
3. That the Secretary to the Sadharan Brahmo Samaj be requested to be kind enough to prepare and send a Draft deed of conveyance and to nominate certain influential persons, members of the Somaj to become trustees in conjunction with Babus Gunabhi Ram Baruah and Sarat Chandra Mazoomdar of this place and also to advise this Somaj as how to proceed in this important matter.

Srimati Bishnupreya Devi, wife of Babu Gunabhi Ram Baruah communicated to them.

Availing of this opportunity it was proposed by Babu Sarat Chandra Mazoomdar and second by Babu Guru Nath Dutta that the following gentlemen be elected members of the Nowgung Brahmo Samaj:

Babu Rajmohan Khasnavis
Babu Bama Prosanna Gupta
Babu Madhu Sudan Gupta
Babu Raghu Nath Baral
Babu Naba Kumar Bisvas

4. Resolved that copies of this day's proceedings be sent to the Editors of the *Brahmo Public Opinion*, and the Tattava Kaumadi with request that they kindly public the same in their papers.

(*Source: Brahmo Public Opinion*, Calcutta, 20 October, 1879.)

APPENDIX H

REPORT ON THE RULES OF NAWGONG (NAGAON) BRAHMO SAMAJ

The following are the Rules of the Nowgong Brahmo Samaj.

1. In this Mandir the only one God in spirit is to be worshipped. No idolatrous anusthans are to take place.
2. Those who believed in the fundamental truths are Brahmoism, are above the age of 18 years and pay a minimum subscription of one Rupee a year, are eligible to be members of the Nowgong Brahmo Samaj. If any person believes in the fundamental truths of Brahmoism and cannot pay the annual subscription but joins the usual prayer meeting, can also be members of this Samaj.
3. None but anusthanik Brahmos can fill the posts of Acharya, Minister and Secretary.
4. Anusthanik members will only be able to give votes in occasions of appointment and dismissal of Acharja and Secretary.
5. All proceedings of the Samaj will be done with reference to the voice of the majority.
6. There is no differences of privilege of resident or non-resident members, the latter will be able to inform the Secretary of their opinion in writing.
7. This Samaj will join the Sadharan Brahmo Samaj of Calcutta in propagating Brahmoism.
8. Babus Gurudas and Padmahash Goswami will be Acharja and Secretary of this Samaj.

9. The two above named gentlemen as well as Babu Sarat Chandra Majumdar will be the members of the managing committee.

30th June, 1878

Padmahash Goswami
Secretary,
Nowgong Brahmo Samaj

(*Source: Brahmo Public Opinion*, 18 July, 1878.)

APPENDIX I

A REPORT ON SOME BRAHMO SAMAJ ACTIVITIES AT SHILLONG (1887)

A friend write from Shillong—Pandit R.K. Vidyaratna arrived here at the latter part of July and worked in our midst for more than three weeks. As he was invited by the Inspector of Schools to attend the educational conference as a non-official member, much of his time was spent in the conference affairs. In the mornings he visited the residents of the station and the evening conducted service at the prayer meetings held at the houses of Brahmos and other.

The last day of July was a day of great rejoicing for the Shillong Brahmos; it was the day on which the new Prayer Hall of the Shillong Brahmo Samaj was consecrated. In the morning there was a Sankirtan procession from the house of the Secretary to the New Mandir. In spite of unfavourable weather, there was a large gathering consisting of people of different sects and the name of the Lord was sung very enthusiastically. After the procession was over there was Divine Service in the Mandir conducted by Pandit Vidyaratna. The service was very impressive, the afternoon was spent in reading and individual prayers. In the evening there was the usual service.

Some of our friends from the plains, who had been invited to attend the conference very heartily joined us and contributed not a little to the success of the consecration ceremony.

The namakaran ceremony of the daughter of Babu Brojendra Nath Sen was performed by the Pandit on 2nd August. The girl was named Ushabala.

(*Source: The Indian Messenger*, 4 September, 1887.)

APPENDIX J

A REPORT ON THE ATROCITIES ON TEA GARDEN WORKERS IN DIBRUGARH DISTRICT, ASSAM

Debrughur, Assam, the 14th November, 1887. As you take great interest in matters connected with cooly life in Assam, I shall feel obliged by your kindly publishing the following communication—

> A batch of emigrants arrivaed here a few days ago; like those coolies whose circumstances require them to be taken on their arrival, before the District Magistrate for orders, this particular batch was, likewise, on landing at Debrughur, taken to the Cutcharry before the Deputy Commissioner. The statements of those poor creatures have created such a sensation that people are doubting whether such things can be possible under the British Government. The batch was composed of three helpless women of respectable class; their names are Ahladi, Shoshi, and Deologni. It was only from the first two that we could gather information as to how they became victims of the slavery Act of the most highly civilized British Government; whereas the last woman Deologni having becoming insane during the Voyage, could tell us nothing about her and the little that could be gathered concerning this woman was only from her two associations.
>
> Ahlady, alias Khanto, is the daughter of Modhu Chuckerbutty, caste Brahmin of village Gopinathpore, Post Office Sheore, District Hugly. So Shashi's father's name was Haradhone Roy, caste Boistob; her home is also at Gopinathpore. Both these women were bathing in the Ganga at the Juggernath Ghat, Calcutta; in course of conversation Alhady told Shoshi that she had a relative somewhere at Burra Bazar whom she would like to see if

she knew the place where he lived. Hearing this, some one near them volunteered to show them the place, and another woman corroborated what this man said. Thereupon the voluntary brought a hackney took Alhady and Shoshi therein, and drove them off. This was at about 10 a.m. after driving from place to place, at last at about 5 p.m. they were brought to a house where they were confined for some 5 or 6 hours and afterwards again put into a coach and brought to the Sealdah Station, where of their utter astonishment, they were locked up in the train which they left for Goalundo and Dhubri. Breaking there journey now by train, and then by steamer, they at last arrived, as they said, at a place (Dhubri), and taken to some houses where they were thrust into the company of innumerable ragged, half-clad dirty men, women and children. The next day they were conducted to the River Ghat, and filed before a Shahib, and then put on board a steamer which after five days arrived at this place (Debrughur), it was on board the steamer that Alhady and Shashi got acquainted with Deologni who told them that she was a Rajput and had two children at home; one day quarrelling with someone at home, she in the heat of anger, came out to the road where she was accosted by a man who, pretending to console her, put her into the train and conveyed to where God knows. Deologni was in her senses but always crying for her children till the second day after they were shipped, when suddenly she became mute and showed sign of insanity. For eleven days they did not eat anything on board the steamer; doctor used to give them sweetmeats which however, they did not take; when disembarking at Debrughur, Deologni suddenly became a tigress, and belaboured the steamer Doctor with kicks and blows. The other day merciful death put an end to all her miseries when it had been arranged to send her down to the Tezpore Lunatic Asylum. The tears of these poor women would move the heart of anybody; they would cling round the legs of anyone who would kindly ask them their circumstances. Our kind hearted Deputy

> Commissioner detained them for some two days till the receipt for their contracts but when these showed nothing to authorize his interference, they were taken to their destination the Khobong Garden in this District.

Mr. Editor in what a deadful time we are living can Government honestly boast of having given us liberty of life and property? Ah who can the effects of the cursed Cooly Act! What innumerable families has it not made, and daily making homeless, helpless and miserable beyond conception causing separation between parents and children, husband and wives, brothers and sisters, will retributive justice recoil up on the authors of the Coolie Act? Our Indian reformers cannot do a more beneficial act than to endeavour to repeal this law. Agitation for it is more needed than for reform in the Legislative Councils changed of Civil Service examination ago and similar questions.

We are proposing to liberate the surviving two women by paying all their recruiting expenses as well as to prosecute the parties by whom they have been brought into trouble. We have enquired and found who was their recruiter. But to effect this, some three to four hundred rupees will be required and we respectfully ask the generous public to subscribe to this laudable object. Subscriptions will be thankfully received by Babu Radhika Churn Miter, B.L. Pleader, Debrughur.

(*Source: The Indian Messenger*, 4 December, 1887.)

APPENDIX K

THE COOLIE QUESTION

"Decoying innocent and genteel people for cooly-work in Assam is becoming painfully frequent. Not long ago the *Sanjibani* gave publication to a case in which some Ranigunge recruiters had taken away four men from their homes on false pretences and were attempting to transport them to Assam unregistered, when they were detected and baffled. A criminal case against them is still pending at Burdwan, without much hope of a successful issue, since the aggrieved themselves for fear of greater zoolum are unwilling to carry the case through and have made themselves scarce. The Mirror hears of two similar cases in which two widowed ladies of genteel birth met with a worse fate and were taken to Dhubri. Their cases are, being investigated at Debrugur, and it is hoped that the miscreants will be punished. It is not enough to hunt up isolated cases, like these. With facts like these before it, the Government can hardly plead that it is not yet time for it to move in the matter. The law requires modifications that will make the recurrence of these cases impossible, or it will be idle to pretend that the British Government does not Labour and encourage slavery. Our public bodies and the question, and it would be well if the National Congress could be made to consider the question, we urged its importance on the Congress held last year, but were told that the question being "purely local" could not be taken up by a national assembly. A more fallacious and absurd position it would be impossible to imagine. Principles of gigantic importance are involved in the consideration of the question and it is idle to call it local because for soothe the people of particular localities alone are the victims of the system. To our mind few questions of practical Indian politics are of a greater imperial interest."

(*Source: Brahmo Public Opinion*, 4 December, 1887.)

APPENDIX L

THE INDIAN ASSOCIATION ON THE COOLIE EMIGRATION ACT

The Committee of the Indian Association have addressed a memorial to the Government of India on the subject of the working of the Coolie Emigration Act of 1882. The committee maintain that the worst apprehensions of the opponents of the Act led by the Late Kristo Das Pal have, judged by the light of subsequent events, been justified and pray for the appointment of a commission to inquire into the condition of the coolies in the Assam tea gardens. To make put the necessity for such a commission of inquiry the committee have directed the attention of Government to several objectionable features of the Act and to the numerous cases of oppression which have resulted therefore. In the first place, the Committee point out the inability of ignorant labourers to protect themselves against the snares of unprincipled recruiters, who by means of false and delusive promises make them enter into contracts the real nature of which they do not understand. The following is one of such cases which have been brought to the notice of the committee:

> Kessur Sing Nepali was a peon attached to the Mungpoo Post Office in the district of Darjeeling, and used to get a salary of Rs.10/- per month. But the work of post peon being of an arduous nature, Kessur Sing in an evil moment thought of resigning his post, it he could recure a better one. Thus with a view to improve his condition, he took leave for a few days and came down to Silliguri. There he met with the brother of one Lutchman Sing Jemadur. Lutchman was described by this man as a person of considerable influence in Assam, who could easily secure for Kessur Sing a suitable appointment on a salary of

Rs.15/- or 20/- per month if he would but go there. The offer was too tempting for Kessur Sing and he had no reason to suspect that he was being decoyed by this recruiter; so he forth with went back to Mungpoo, resigned his appointment there, and having secured from the post-master a certificate of good character efficiency, he returned to Silliguri with his wife. From Silliguri the party came down to Jalpiguri, where they met Luchman Sing, who took from them Rs.5/ as their railway fare, and brought them to Dhubri, where they lodge in the Coolie depot. Kessur Sing on solemn affirmation stated before the Deputy Commissioner of Darrang, that, soon after they were lodged in the depot, "a Babu took down our names and gave us a blanket, two coortas (shirt) and two dhooties and a tin mug. I did not wish to accept these things, but the Jemadar Lutchman Sing said they were given us as present by the Sirkar and returned me the Rs.5/-. I had given as my railway fare. We got no other money and this was my own. I never saw any agreement and I never signed any agreement. I can sign my own name. No saheb asked me any question. A saheb came on horse back to the depot once, but left without saying anything. It was not till I got on board the steamer when the doctor said you must drink here and not there, that I found out I was an emigrant." There was an exciting scene on board the steamer, where Kessur Sing refused to drink water drawn from the river by the Mahamedan crew. It was difficult to persuade Kessur Sing to give up his Caste and the incident of his refusal created no small commotion. A gentleman, who was a passenger on board the steamer having been drawn to the scene of the tumult and having acquainted himself with all the particulars of the case, felt interested in it. When the steamer reached Tezpur, Kessur and his wife were landed on shore. The gentleman followed them to the coolie depot, where they were lodged for the night. Having thus ascertained the place, he went to a kind-hearted pleader of the town and gave him all particulars of the case. The pleader was good enough to take up the cause of poor Kessur Sing and his wife. He went to the Deputy Commissioner's house and instituted a suit for their release. The Deputy Commissioner made a reference to the Deputy Commissioner of Dhubri on the subject and on the receipt of his reply passed on the 10th of August, 1886 the following order on the petition of Kessur Sing and his wife:

No. 1005

Order of the Deputy Commissioner of Darrang passed on the petition of Kessur Sing Nepali and Mussamud Rupkanotee. Read letter 266E dated 7th August from the Deputy Commissioner, Dhubri. From the statements contained in this letter it is quite clear Kessur Sing and his wife entered into agreements and petition to the effect he was deceived can not be entertained. He must therefore proceed to the garden for which he was recruited.

Dated: 11-8-86

Sd/-
A.E. Campbell
Deputy Commissioner
Darrang

The committee next proceed to draw the attention of government to the miserable life which coolies have to lead when they arrive in the tea gardens. How hard is their lot will be evident from the following quotation from the report of Dr. Eteson, Deputy Surgeon General and Sanitary Commissioner of Assam.

The condition of the emigrant labourer alters greatly for the worse immediately he is landed from river steamer and discharged from the Government sanitary protection. In many important respects he is thenceforward left to his own resources; in other he receives only modified and often injudicious care; in all the conditions of life he is less favourably placed than before. His food is no longer dietetic and carefully cooked; his clothing and bedding (beyond a blanket) is left to himself to provide; his lodging is often inadequate against the variations of climate; his works exposes him to all weathers, and often to dangerous disease causes; he is unprotected against drinking to excess; may he is in many instances, almost tempted to it; even if he falls ill, the hospital is a name only, he may receive medicine either by daily attendance at a dispensary or given to him in his hut; but the care, suitable food, adequate restoratives and nursing are, generally speaking, unknown.

It is no wonder therefore that the rate of sickness and mortality among the tea-garden labourers as a class has been always very great; that in many gardens it is above what is counted a frightful epidemic in civilised countries; and the subject has been an unceasing anxiety to the Government of province.

But if such is the condition of adult life in the Assam tea-gardens, the conditions of the child-life are still more terrible. The rate of mortality among the coolie children is simply appalling. In 1884 the death rate among children in tea-gardens had risen from 39.7 to 44 per thousand. While the death rate incrèased the birth rate gradually fell; in 1882 it was 39.7 per thousand; in 1883 it was 34.3 and in 1884 it further decreased to 32.7 per thousand.

The Chief Commissioner of Assam accounts for this excessive mortality, in the following manner:

> Neglect on the part of the women who are unable to do their daily task and at the same time look after the children and who can not afford to do no work and stay at home accounts in a great measure for the high mortality among children.
>
> The difficulty of working hard in the tea-gardens and of nursing new born off springs at one and the same time is such that "coolie women frequently have recourses to abortion and Dais (midwives) who procure it often make their business a profitable one."

The committee next call the attention of Government to the oppressive treatment of coolies by planters and mention several instances of such oppression. We regret, we have no space to make one or two extracts of such cases. A strong prima facie case, has in our opinion, been made out for the appointment of a commissioner of inquiry and we hope Lord Dufferin's Government will lose no time in granting the request of the Indian Association. Even the *Pioneer* is in favour of a commission of inquiry, although the *Englishman*, as an organ of the tea planters, is naturally opposed to it. The allegations made in the memorial of the Indian Association are, if true simply scandalous and should be carefully inquired into without delay.

(*Source: The Indian Messenger*, 27 May, 1888.)

APPENDIX M

REPORT ON COOLIE DEPOTS IN CALCUTTA

Information has reached us that there are in Calcutta several coolie depots, where often times parties who have been decoyed by the Assam recruiters by false hopes are forcibly confined against their will. These depots, we believe, are not unknown to the police, nor are the police ignorant of some of the cases which have occurred in this connection, and the details of which we purposely refrain from mentioning now. But surely depots of this kind, where people sometimes forcibly confined ought not to be permitted to exist in Calcutta above all places, and those who have anything to do with them ought to be traced out and punished. We beg to call Sir Henry Harrison's attention to this matter.

(*Source: The Indian Messenger*, 11 December, 1887.)

APPENDIX N

LIST OF BRAHMO SAMAJES IN (UNDIVIDED) ASSAM, 1877

1. Goalpara	1870
2. Gauhati	1870
3. Nowgong	1870
4. Shillong	1875
5. Sibsagar	1866
6. Tezpur	1870
7. Dhubri	1875

APPENDIX O

LIST OF BRAHMO SAMAJES IN (UNDIVIDED) ASSAM, 1889

Name of the place	Year of establishment
Cachar 1. B.S.	1865
2. Silchar	
Dibrugarh B.S.	1887
Dibru B.S.	1875
Golaghat B.S.	1886
Gauhati B.S.	1870
Jasir B.S. Via Shella (Khasi Hills)	1889
Lait Kynsew (Khasi Hills)	1891
Mowkhar B.S. Via Shillong (Khasi Hills)	1886
Mawrynkhong B.S. (Khasi Hills)	1889
Mousmai B.S. Via Cheraponji (Khasi Hills)	1889
Nowgong B.S.	1879
Nongrim (Khasi Hills)	1890
Shillong B.S.	1874
Shibsagar B.S. (Revived)	1880
Sunamganj Students' Weekly Service	
Sylhet 1. B.S.	1861
2. Students' Samaj	1879
Tezpur B.S.	1872

APPENDIX P

BOARD OF TRUSTEES OF GAUHATI BRAHMO SAMAJ

1916 **First Board of Trustees**
Sarat Chandra Das
Heramba Chandra Maitra
Dr. Prankrishna Acharya
Gurudas Chakravorty
Rai Saheb Raj Mohon Das
Sibnath Dutta
Prasanna Chandra Das Gupta
Abhoy Charan Das

1940 **Second Board of Trustees**
Lolit Mohan Das
Satish Chandra Das
Probodh Kumar Lahiri
Rajendra Chandra Sarkar
Girija Kumar Das
Amar Chandra Bhattacharjee
Birendra Chandra Chakravorty

1958 **Third Board of Trustees**
Prabhat Kumar Das
Kiranmoy Lahiri
Subimal Das
Braja Gopal Halder
Sisir Kumar Deb
Dr. Amalendu Sen
Ajay Sen
Anjali Lahiri

1995 **Fourth Board of Trustees**
Anjali Lahiri
Pushpalata Das

	Minati Chanda
	Dr. B.R. Halder
2000	**Present Board of Trustees**
	Anjali Lahiri
	Pushpalata Das
	Minati Chania
	Dr. B.R. Halder
	Krishnanjan Chanda
	Rukma Sen
	Dr. Ardhendu Banerjee
	Dr. Dipankar Banerjee
	Dr. Mukti Deb Choudhury
	Sheila Dutta*

*During 2005-06, Bipash Ranjan Halder, Samarendra Nath Das and Ashoke Chowdhury were co-opted in the Board of Trustees of Gauhati Brahmo Samaj.

APPENDIX Q

BOARD OF TRUSTEES OF SHILLONG BRAHMO SAMAJ (1874-2006)

1. SHILLONG BRAHMO SAMAJ

   Trustees: From 1874-1900 Approx.
   Rai Bahadur Prakash Chandra Deb
   Brojendra Nath Sen
   Aukhoy Kumar Chatterjee
   Sadaya Charan Das
   Rai Bahadur Sivnath Dutta

2. SHILLONG BRAHMO SAMAJ/KHASI HILLS BRAHMO SAMAJ

   Trustees: Between 1902-1935 Approx.
   Raj Chandra Choudhury
   Rai Saheb Sivnath Dutta
   Brojendra Nath Sen
   Rev. Nilmoni Chakraborty
   Lal Madhab Bose
   Rai Bahadur Mahendra Kumar Gupta

U Radhon Singh Berry Babu Jeevon Roy Babu Job Solomon	Mawkhar Brahmo Samaj— Under Shillong Brahmo Samaj from about 1900-1903

3. SHILLONG BRAHMO SAMAJ/KHASI HILLS BRAHMO SAMAJ

   Trustees: Between 1937-1950 Approx.
   Rai Saheb Sivnath Dutta
   Jyotirendranath Das
   Anath Bandhu Sen
   Atulananda Das
   Girish Chandra Bhattacharjee
   Sarada Manjari Dutta

Abhinash Chandra Dutta
Rai Bahadur Mahendra Kumar Gupta

4. SHILLONG BRAHMO SAMAJ/KHASI HILLS BRAHMO SAMAJ

   Trustees: Between 1960-2004 Approx.
   Dr. Robi Chanda
   Mrs. Sushama Roy
   Mrs. Jyotirmoy Gupta
   Mrs. Suvarnaprova Das
   Rajya Ratna Mr. S.V. Mukherjee
   Miss Sushila Sen
   Mrs. Madhuri Chanda
   Mr. Subrata Dutta
   Mr. Ranjit Das

5. SHILLONG BRAHMO SAMAJ/KHASI HILLS BRAHMO SAMAJ

   Trustees: From 2004 to date
   Mr. Subrata Dutta
   Mr. Barun Kumar Roy
   Mr. Raja Surajit Sen
   Mr. Biswajit Dutta
   Mr. Surojit Dutta

APPENDIX R

FASCIMILE OF 1908 TRUST DEED OF GAUHATI BRAHMO SAMAJ

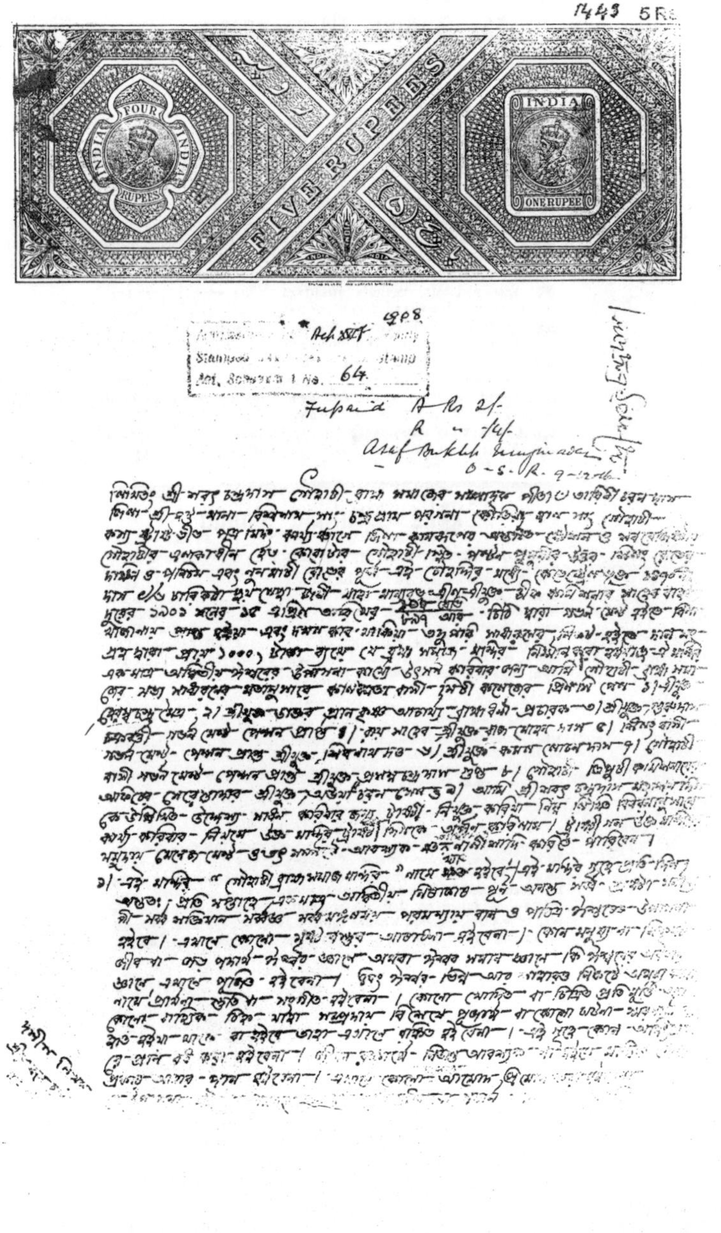

APPENDIX S

REPORT OF THE "WEB CASE" IN THE INDIAN MESSENGER

The Indian Messenger

...ration of Native States. In th...
retrenchment appears to have been ...
though we are not inclined to b...
drawing Rs. 15 per month has bee...

In the *Indian ...or* of Thursday last appears the following telegram:—"A European is in trouble. Mr. C. Webb, Agent, Koklamukh, is accused of rape, wrongful confinement, &c. A batch of coolies bound for Holangurie arrived at the Mukh before evening. Amongst them was a young woman. She attracted Mr. Webb's attention. The coolies were permitted to stay for the night on the flat, a part of which forms his quarters. Enticements failing, the young woman was forced into his room. Her husband resisting, got a sound caning, and could not prevent the outrage. She was in Mr. Webb's room the whole night, shrieking. Next morning, she complained of pain in the abdomen. She died after reaching Holangurie of looseness of bowels. The case is pending in the Assistant Commissioner's Court, Jorehat. Both Europeans and Natives evince great concern for the result."—! !

The Brahmo Samaj

A Brahmo marriage according t... ...as celebrated here on the 26th April l... ...is Babu Dwarakanath Chakravarti, a railway... ...Railway, and widower; and the bride Sr... ...undari Devi, lately teacher of the Barakpur gi... ...a widow. The age of the bridegroom is about 40, and of the bride about 20. Both are Brahmins by caste.

We beg to acknowledge with thanks, on behalf of the Executive Committee, Sadharan Brahmo Samaj, the receipt of a donation of Rs. 20 for charitable purposes, from a Brahma friend at Lahore, who does not wish his name to be published, and one of Rs. 5 from a widow lady of Bikrampur.

We are very sorry to learn, that Pandit S. N. Agnihotri has been compelled to return to Lahore leaving Pandit Sivanath Sastri to work alone. From the day of his joining the latter at Giridih, he has been keeping indifferent health. For some time past he has been suffering from an inflamation of the eyes, and other complaints—so much so that, on account of this failing health, the idea of visiting Ranchi, whence there was an urgent and pressing invitation, had to be given up. But in spite of this failing health,

APPENDIX T

REPORT OF RAMKUMAR VIDYARATNA'S ASSAM VISIT IN THE INDIAN MESSENGER

THE

Indian Messenger.

A WEEKLY JOURNAL,

MAINLY DEVOTED TO RELIGIOUS, SOCIAL, MORAL AND EDUCATIONAL TOPICS,

PUBLISHED EVERY SUNDAY MORNING.

Vol. I. No. 34. CALCUTTA:—SUNDAY, MAY 4, 1884. ***Per Annum in Advance.* Town and Mofussil Rupees 4.**

We have been favoured with the following account (translated from the Bengali) of Pandit Ramkumar Vidyaratna's recent . Assam:—

d Lakshmipur on the 8th Chaitra last. This before this visit any Brahma Mis- copped here for three days, Babu the house of our friend, deliv sed the local students one day on oceeded to a place called Agia where Chatterji lives. No other gentleman ... meeting consisting of a number of poor people, and explained to them the principles of Brahmoism. Thence I proceeded to Goalpara where I stopped for three days (from 15th to 17th Chaitra) and delivered three public lectures and had prayers with a number of friends. From Goalpara I went to Barapeta. The way to this place is very painful—lying through a dense jungle extending through ten miles at the further end of which lies the village of Barapeta. On my way there, I had to walk all the way, and met with several wild animals, but by the grace of God, none of them could touch me. Barapeta is the sacred place of the *Mahapurushiyas* and is inhabited by eleven thousand souls, a number which is not to be found in any of our villages. I delivered three public lectures here; one near a garden where some 500 people were present, another at the local school, and the last at the *Shastra*, that is, the prayer-hall of the *Mahapurushyas*, where about a thousand people attended. The received me very cordially and presented me with provisions white garments as marks of respect. My lectures here m the Government officers also show much kindness to me. T place had not been, before this, visited by me or any other missio I have now reached Gauhati. I shall inform you hereafter of work here and my subsequent movements!

THE THIRD ANNIVERSARY OF THE BOMBAY BRAHMA SAMAJ.—The third anniversary of this Samaj, which fell on Saturday the 1th instant, was celebrated on that day and on the Sunday following at the residence of Babu Akshayakumar Mitra. On Saturday there was morning service in Hindi, by Babu Akshayakumar Mitra who in the course of it preached a concise but sweet and impressive sermon on the subject of "Bhawasagar" or the world-ocean. He said that this was a treacherous and mysterious deep, impossible for man to cross by his own power, and tenanted by dreadful sea-monsters—the six passions—which it was very difficult to avoid. Nothing, said he, but divine guidance and help which must be sought through faith, devotion and love can deliver us from this danger. The same evening there was service in Marathi which was conducted by Mr. Sadashiv Pandurang Kelkar. In his sermon he impressed on his hearers the necessity of carrying with them their religious experiences and their good work of the previous year to the annual Utsavas to be able to participate to the full in the enjoyment of such festivities. Sunday morning was appointed for a lecture on "*Brahmadharma*" of F Brahmos. This was delivered by Mr. Yashwant F Manerikar. He introduced the subject by telling that India was the mother-land of religions and glory was her religious glory. After giving a brief present theistic movement of India he entered f the fundamental principles of t ...th and

APPENDIX U

NILMANI CHAKRAVARTY

APPENDIX V

GUNABHIRAM BARUAH

APPENDIX W

BRAHMO SAMAJ, SHILLONG

BIBLIOGRAPHY

PRIMARY SOURCES

(A) Official Records, Reports and Proceedings (Unpublished and Published)

1. Report on the Administration of the Province of Assam for the year 1874-75 and 1875-76.
2. Summary of Education Reports, Public Instruction Department, Eastern Bengal and Assam, 1901.
3. Proceedings of the Chief Commissioner of Assam in the Notification, General Dept. No. 3831/1/2G dated July 4, 1890.
4. Assam Secretariat Reports, Revenue Proceedings A January 1879, No. 26.
5. Home (A) Proceedings of Chief Commissioner of Assam, No. 32-52, February 1902.
6. Report on the Land Revenue Administration of the Lower province, 1870-71, Govt. of Bengal, Calcutta, 1872.
7. Report of the Commissioner of Upper Assam on Tea Estates, British Parliamentary Papers, 1867.

(B) Newspapers and Periodicals

English

Brahmo Public Opinion, Calcutta
Golden Jubilee Souvenir, Lady Keane Girls' College, Shillong
Indian Messenger (The), Calcutta
Perspective, Guwahati
Purbasree, Silchar
Race and Ryots, Calcutta
Shillong Times (The), Golden Jubilee Souvenir, Shillong
Telegraph (The), Calcutta
Times of Assam (The)

Vernacular (Assamese and Bengali)

Assam Bandhu
Awahan, Calcutta
Banhi, Calcutta and then Delhi
Bengalee, Calcutta
Dacca Prakash, Dacca
Digvijaya, Dibrugarh
Eka ebong Koekjon, Guwahati
Gyanada, Calcutta
Jonaki
Orunodoi, Guwahati
Sanhriti, Shillong
Sanjivani, Calcutta
Somprakash, Changripota

(C) Interviews

1. Interview with nonagenarian Susama Roy, who resides at Laban Shillong.
2. Interview with Anjali Lahiri, granddaughter of Sarada Manjari Devi (now octogenarian), Social Worker and Author, based at Guwahati.
3. Interview with Indira Khusalini, daughter of Broja Sundar Roy in 1984, when she was residing at 48 Park Street, Kolkata.
4. Interview with Nirupama Bargohain, noted litterateur and novelist of Assam.

SECONDARY SOURCES

(A) Books

English

Andrews, C.F., *The Renaissance of India* (London, 1912)
Barpujari, H.K. (ed.), *The Comprehensive History of Assam*, Vol. V (Guwahati, 1993)
Bose, S.K., *Capital and Labour in Indian Tea Industry* (Bombay, 1954)

Chandra Bipan, *Rise and Growth of Economic Nationalism in India* (New Delhi, 1991)

Chandra Sudhir, *The Oppressive Present: Literature and Consciousness in Colonial India* (New Delhi, 1994)

Chattopadhaya, Gautam, *Communism and Bengal's Freedom Movement*, Vol. I (New Delhi, 1970)

Chattopadhaya, Ramananda, *Rammohan Roy and Modern India* (Calcutta, 1918)

Cotton, Sir Henry, *Indian and Home Memories* (London, 1911)

Fuller, Sir Bampfylde, *Some Personal Experience* (London, 1930)

Ganguly, Dwarakanath, *Slavery in British Dominion* (Calcutta, 1972)

Griffiths, P., *The History of the Tea Industry* (London, 1967)

Guha, Amalendu, *Planter Raj to Swaraj* (New Delhi, 1979)

Hunter, W.W., *Statistical Account of Assam*, 1998.

Kopf, David, *The Brahmo Samaj and the Shaping of the Modern Indian Mind* (Princeton, 1979)

Misra, Tilottama, *Literature and Society in Assam* (Guwahati, 1987)

Misra, Udayan, *The Transformation of Assams Identity: A Historical Survey* (Shillong, 2001)

Pal, Bipin Chandra, *Memories of My Life and Times*, Vol. I (Calcutta, 1932)

Pal, Bipin Chandra, *Beginning of the Freedom Movement in India* (Calcutta, 1959)

Ratter, Rev. M.C., *To Nangroi* (London, 1932)

Roy, Lakshmi Narayan (ed.), *Brahmo Samaj, Depressed Classes and Untouchability* (Calcutta, 1996)

Saikia, Rajen, *Social and Economic History of Assam* (1853-1921), (New Delhi, 2001)

Sastri, Sivanath, *History of Brahmo Samaj* (Calcutta, 1993)

Sen, Sukomol, *Working Class of India, History of Emergence and Movement* (Calcutta, 1977)

Singh, K.S., *Tribal Movements in India*, Vol. II (New Delhi, 1982)

Spencer Lavan, *Unitarians and India, A Study in Encounter and Response* (Chicago, 1991)

Assamese

Ahmed, Gairika Baruah, *Heroa Bahir Sur*, Guwahati, 2005
Barman, Kashinath, *Nari Ratna* (Guwahati, 1986)
Barman, Sivnath, *Asamiya Jibani Abhidhan* (Guwahati, 1992)
Barpujari, H.K., *Asamor Naba Jagaran, Ana Asamiyar Bhumika* (Jorhat, 1983)
Barua, Gunabhiram, *Anandaram Dhekial Phukanar Jiban Charita* (Guwahati, 1971)
Barua, Prafulla Chandra, *Asamat Batori Kakat: Eti Rooprekha* (Guwahati, 1993)
Bezbarua, Lakshminath, *Mor Jiwan Sonwaran* (Dibrugarh, 1998)
Bhuyan, Jogendra Narayan, *Uoli Joa Nathir Pora* (Nogaon, 1991)
Bora, Hem, *Asamiya Sahitya Loi Mohila Lekhakar Dan* (Golaghat, 1994)
Borthakur, Shiela, *Lekhikar Jibani* (Guwahati, 1987)
Choudhury, Prasenjit, *Asamer Cha Banua aru Unabingsho Satikar Vidyat Samaj* (Dibrugarh, 1989)
Gohain Barua, Padmanath (ed.), *Jivani Sangraha* (Guwahati)
Hazarika, Atul Chandra (ed.), *Bezbarua Granthabali*, Vol. II (Guwahati, 1968)
Misra, Tilottama, *Swarnalata* (Guwahati, 1997)
Saikia, Chandra Prasad (ed.), *Radhanath Chengkakoti* (Guwahati, 1971)
Saikia, Chandra Prasad (ed.), *Lakshminath Bezbarua* (Guwahati, 1968)
Talukdar, Nanda, *Jivan Swaran* (Guwahati, 1981)
Talukdar, Nonda, *Sambad Patrar Kancriali Rodat Asamiya Sahitya* (Guwahati, 1975)

Bengali

Basu, Rajnarayan, *Atmacharit* (Calcutta)
Bhattacharjee, Jatindra Mohan (ed.), *Ramnavami Natak* (Calcutta, 1372 B.S.)

Chakraborty, Ajit Kumar, *Maharshi Devendra Nath Thakur* (Calcutta, 1971)
Chakraborty, Nilmoni, *Atmajivansmriti* (Calcutta, 1382 B.S.)
Chakraborty, Satish Chandra, *Sivanath Sastri* (Calcutta, 1375 B.S.)
Chattopadhaya, Kanailal, *Asame Cha Coolie Andolon O Ramkumar Vidyaratna* (Calcutta, 1989)
Dutta, Amar, *Asame Cha Coolie Andolon O Dwarakanath* (Calcutta, 1978)
Dutta, Saradamanjari, *Mahajatrar Pathey* (Calcutta, 1348 B.S.)
Ganguly, Prabhat Chandra, *Bharater Rastrio Itihaser Khasra* (Calcutta, 1960)
Sastri, Sivanath, *Ramtanu Lahiri O Tatkalin Bonga Samaj* (Calcutta, 1903)
Sastri, Sivanath, *Sadhanasramer Itibritto* (Calcutta, 1992)
Sastri, Sivanath, *Atmacharita* (Calcutta, 1940)
Sen, Sukumar, *Bangla Sahityer Itihas* (Calcutta, 1377 B.S.)
Sen Gupta, Pradyut, *Banglar Sramik Jiban O Natya Sahitya* (Calcutta, 1976)
Tagore, Devendra Nath, *Atmajibani* (Calcutta, 1968)
Vidyaratna, Ramkumar, *Udasin Satyasrabar Assam Bhraman*
(Unknown author), *Assam Bhraman* (Calcutta, 1893)

(B) Booklets

English

Brahmo Prarthana Samajes in India, published by Andhra Brahmo Samaj and Hyderabad Deccan Brahmo Samaj, Hyderabad, 1996.

Bengali

Lahiri, Anjali, *Subama Prava Das ebong Tatkalin Nari Samaj* (Shillong)
Mukherjee, Sudhir, *Mahapran Ramesh Ch. Mukherjee* (Calcutta, 1956)

Mahapran Atul Chandra Roy, Sradhanjali (Calcutta, 1940)
Bhakta Sadhak Mathuranath Nandi, Jivani Prasanga, Sadharan Brahmo Samaj (Calcutta)

(C) Unpublished Thesis

Banerjee, D., Labour Unrest in Assam: Some Aspects of the Labour Movement Among Non-Plantation workers (M.Phil. Dissertation, JNU), 1984.

(D) Journals/Proceedings/Volumes

Proceeding Volumes of North-East India History Association, Select issues
Indian Economic and Social History Review
Report of the Indian Association, select issues
Report of the Indian National Congress, 1896
Different Leaflets of Sadharan Brahmo Samaj

INDEX